FIFTH EDITION

The
iPhone

How to do the most important,
useful & fun stuff with your iPhone

Book

Scott Kelby & Terry White

The iPhone Book, Fifth Edition

The iPhone Book Team

CREATIVE DIRECTOR
Felix Nelson

TRAFFIC DIRECTOR
Kim Gabriel

PRODUCTION MANAGER
Dave Damstra

TECHNICAL EDITORS
Kim Doty
Cindy Snyder

ART DIRECTOR
Jessica Maldonado

PUBLISHED BY
Peachpit Press

Copyright © 2012 by Scott Kelby

Composed in Myriad Pro, Helvetica Neue, and Helvetica by Kelby Media Group.

Trademarks
All terms mentioned in this book that are known to be trademarks or service marks have been appropriately capitalized. Peachpit Press cannot attest to the accuracy of this information. Use of a term in the book should not be regarded as affecting the validity of any trademark or service mark.

iPhone, iPod, iTunes, iPad, Macintosh, and Mac are registered trademarks of Apple. Windows is a registered trademark of Microsoft Corporation.

Warning and Disclaimer
This book is designed to provide information about the iPhone. Every effort has been made to make this book as complete and as accurate as possible, but no warranty of fitness is implied.

The information is provided on an as-is basis. The authors and Peachpit Press shall have neither liability nor responsibility to any person or entity with respect to any loss or damages arising from the information contained in this book or from the use of the discs or programs that may accompany it.

ISBN: 13: 978-0-321-83276-4
ISBN: 10:   0-321-83276-0

9 8 7 6 5 4 3 2 1

Printed and bound in the United States of America

http://kelbytraining.com
www.peachpit.com

PRODUCED BY

Kelbymedia
GROUP INC.

For my wonderful son, Jordan.
It is absolutely a blast being your dad!
–SCOTT KELBY

For my mom, who always taught me to do the right thing,
and for my dad, who inspired me and pushed me to succeed.
I also dedicate this book to Steve Jobs. If it were not for his
vision and determination, the iPhone and many other
tech gifts that enhance our lives would not exist.
–TERRY WHITE

Scott's Acknowledgments

This is the sixth book I've been lucky enough to co-author with Terry, and I can tell you from experience that the only downside of co-authoring a book with him is that I only get half as much space to thank all the wonderful people whose help, hard work, and support go into making a book like this.

To Kalebra: My wonderful, amazing, hilarious, fun-filled, super-gorgeous, and loving wife. Your spirit, warmth, beauty, brains, patience, and unconditional love continue to prove what everybody always says—I'm the luckiest guy in the world.

To Jordan & Kira: You two bring immeasurable joy to my life, and I'm so proud and tickled to be your dad. I couldn't ask for anything more.

To Jeff: You are the world standard that all brothers should be judged by. No wonder everybody loves you the way they do!

To my co-author Terry White: You're the one who convinced me to do this book, and without your many ideas, your influence, and your great writing, this book would never have seen the light of day. I'm truly honored to have shared these pages with you, and to count you among my very best friends.

To Kathy Siler (my secret weapon): Without you, I'd be sitting in my office, mumbling and staring at the ceiling. Thanks for doing all the "hard work," and making my work life have calm, order, and sense, and for making it all a lot of fun. You are the best.

To my editor Kim Doty: I just love working with you. How can you not love working with some-one who always has such a warm smile, such a great attitude, and does such great work? Thanks doesn't cover it…but…thanks.

To Cindy Snyder and Jessica Maldonado (my book editing, design, and layout team): I just love working with you guys, and I'm constantly impressed and amazed at the quality of what you do and how quickly you can do it.

To Felix Nelson, my brilliant Creative Director: What can I say? You are the best in the business and ideas and art flow out of you like a Pez dispenser. I'm a very lucky guy to even get to work with you. Thank you, my friend, for everything you do for me and our company.

To Dave Moser: Getting to work with my best buddy every day is definitely a blessing, but the way you're always looking out for me takes it to a whole new level. :-)

To Jean A. Kendra: Thanks for watching "the other side" of our business and for being such a great friend over the years.

To Nancy Aldrich-Ruenzel, Ted Waitt, Sara Jane Todd, Scott Cowlin, and all my friends at Peachpit Press: Thank you for making the book-writing process virtually painless, and for having me as one of your authors.

To John Graden, Jack Lee, Dave Gales, Judy Farmer, and Douglas Poole: Your wisdom and whip-cracking have helped me immeasurably throughout my life, and I'm both grateful and totally in your debt.

To God and His Son Jesus Christ: Thank You for always hearing my prayers, for always being there when I need You, for blessing me with such a wonderful, joy-filled life, and such a warm, loving family to share it with.

Terry's Acknowledgments

It's not every day that I get to work on a project that is both challenging and fun at the same time. Writing a book such as this takes a lot of focus and attention to detail. Although there were many late nights and much time spent away from my family, they didn't complain once. I have an amazing wife who knows that one of my passions is technology and gadgets, so she completely understood when I said, "Hey, guess what? I'm going to co-author *The iPhone Book* with Scott!" Carla is my balance and she helps me in so many ways every day.

I have two amazing daughters: Ayoola is both smart and constantly focused on taking it to the next level. I see so much of myself in her at times that it's scary. My youngest daughter, Sala, has many of my other traits. She makes me laugh out loud every day and lives to enjoy life. They make those late nights, weekends spent working, and hectic travel schedules worthwhile, because at the end of the day, it's all for them anyway.

I have a great sister, Pam, who is the person I go to when I need advice. It's great having an older sibling and she's the best sister a guy could have.

I have to thank all my "gadget buddies"! It's the guys and gals that I hang out with that inspire me to play and learn about gadgets of all kinds. My colleague Dave Helmly is probably more of a gadget freak than I am. Nine out of 10 times, when I call him to tell him about a new toy, he's already got one in his hands and starts telling me about it. My buddy Larry Becker is always calling me and letting me in on the latest gadget that he just heard about or got to play with. Special thanks to Jack Beckman and Chita Hunter for some last minute hot tips, and to Sarah K for always keeping me up to date with the latest tunes and apps that I may have missed. Speaking of apps, I have to thank both my co-authors on www.bestappsite.com, Erik Bernskiold and Jason Lykins, because I couldn't do it without their help.

If technology is my first passion, then I would have to say that photography is my second. While the iPhone is my go-to device for daily communications and social networking, I also use it and my iPad quite extensively in my photography workflows. With that said, I can't help but thank those individuals that I work with and photograph on a regular basis, starting with the amazing Kandice Lynn. She's a blast to work with and she inspires me to push my photography further. I also want to thank Iris Pérez, Lena Hakim, Bruce Mandel, and Don Pham, as well as all the photography industry leaders that have shown me so much support over the years.

Also, I thank my friends at my local Apple Store: Linda, Carol, and Dave for constantly making me feel like a VIP when I walk in. And, of course, I have to thank all my friends who support me at my Macintosh users' group, MacGroup-Detroit, especially Mary, Joe, Calvin, Jack, Chita, Phyllis, Yvonne, Bill, Brian & Char, Mia, Michele, Steve, Mike, Aquil, and Harold.

Although I enjoy writing, it's not my full-time gig. I have the best job on the planet and work for the best company in the world. I have to give special thanks to my boss, Scott Morris, who understands my gadget addictions and gives me the freedom and the time off that I need to pursue my other technology and industry passions. I work with some of the smartest people in the industry, and I want to thank everyone at Adobe Systems, Inc., including my travel buddies, Worldwide Evangelists Jason Levine and Greg Rewis, not only for providing the best software tools in existence but also for keeping me technically educated and motivated to achieve greatness.

Of course, I have to thank the guy who is probably my biggest source of inspiration, and that is one of my best friends and the co-author of this book, Scott Kelby. I'm constantly amazed at how much this guy accomplishes each year. There is no stopping him. Not only is he great in his career, but he's also a great father to his two beautiful kids and a great husband to his wonderful wife, Kalebra. I probably wouldn't have gotten into all this writing if it wasn't for Scott. Scott, you're an inspiration to us all! Thanks, buddy!

About the Authors

Scott Kelby

Scott is Editor-in-Chief and Publisher of *Photoshop User* magazine, and co-host of *The Grid*, the weekly talk show for photographers. He is President and co-founder of the National Association of Photoshop Professionals (NAPP), the trade association for Adobe® Photoshop® users, and President of the software, education, and publishing firm Kelby Media Group.

Scott is a photographer, designer, and award-winning author of more than 50 books on technology and digital imaging, including the best-selling books: *The iPod Book*, *The Digital Photography Book*, volumes 1, 2, and 3, and *The Photoshop Book for Digital Photographers*. Scott has authored several best-selling Macintosh books, including the award-winning *Macintosh: The Naked Truth*, from New Riders, and *The Mac OS X Leopard Book* and *Mac OS X Killer Tips* from Peachpit Press. His books have been translated into dozens of different languages, including Russian, Chinese, French, German, Spanish, Korean, Greek, Turkish, Japanese, Dutch, and Taiwanese, among others.

For six years straight, Scott was awarded the distinction of being the world's No. 1 best-selling author of all computer and technology books, across all categories and most recently, he was named the #1 best-selling author of books on photography. His book, *The Digital Photography Book*, volume 1, is the best-selling book on digital photography of all time.

Scott is Training Director for the Adobe Photoshop Seminar Tour, Conference Technical Chair for the Photoshop World Conference & Expo, and is a speaker at trade shows and events around the world. For more information on Scott, visit his daily blog at www.scottkelby.com.

Terry White

Terry is the author of *Secrets of Adobe Bridge* from Adobe Press and co-author of *InDesign CS/CS2 Killer Tips*, from New Riders.

Terry is Worldwide Creative Suite Design Evangelist for Adobe Systems, Inc., and has been with Adobe for over a decade, where he leads the charge in evangelizing and showing Adobe's Creative Suite products to users around the world. Terry is both an Adobe Certified Expert and Creative Suite Master.

He has been active in the industry for over 25 years and is the founder and President of MacGroup-Detroit, Michigan's largest Macintosh users' group, and is a columnist for *Photoshop User* magazine.

Terry is the host of the top-ranked *Adobe Creative Suite Video Podcast* (http ://creativesuitepodcast.com) and author of the world renown *Best App Site* (your source for iPhone, iPad, and iPod touch app news and reviews; www .bestappsite.com), *Terry White's Tech Blog* (http://terrywhite.com), and is a key presenter at major industry shows around the world.

Chapter Three   51

Message in a Bottle
Sending Text Messages

Chapter Four   69

App Anthem
Using Apps & the App Store

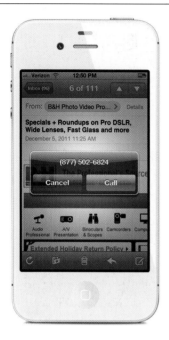

http://kelbytraining.com

Chapter Twelve   221
Video Killed the Radio Star
Using the Videos App

Chapter Thirteen   231
One Hour Photo
Using Your Camera and Working with Photos and Videos

http://kelbytraining.com

Chapter Fourteen   263
Cereal Killer
Killer Tips and Tricks

Chapter Fifteen   293
Setting Me Off
The Ins and Outs of Your iPhone's Settings

The Trouble with Boys
Troubleshooting Your iPhone

http://kelbytraining.com

Seven Things You'll Wish You Had Known...

(1) The first chapter is for people brand new to the iPhone (you just opened the box), so if you've had your iPhone for a few weeks and you already know how to turn it on, how to zoom in, how to get around, put it to sleep, etc., you can skip right over to Chapter 2 and start there. It won't hurt our feelings one bit (but you might want to at least skim through Chapter 1 anyway. Hey, ya never know).

(2) You don't have to read it chapter by chapter. Outside of that first I-just-opened-the-box chapter, we designed this to be a "jump-in-anywhere" book. You don't have to read it in order, chapter by chapter—if you want to learn how to do a certain thing, just find it in the Table of Contents, turn to that page, and you'll have the answer in seconds. Each page shows you how to do just one important thing. One topic. One idea. For example, if you want to learn how to delete an email, we will show you, step by step, how to do exactly that. No big discussions about email account protocols, or about server-side instructions—just how to delete an email message. That's it.

(3) We didn't totally "geek out." Terry and I wrote everything just as if a friend came over to our house, pulled out their new iPhone, and started asking questions. So, for example, if you were at my house and you turned to me and said, "Hey Scott, is there a way to see more of this webpage on my screen?" I wouldn't go into how the iPhone's built-in vibrotactile actuator works. In real life, I'd turn to you and say, "Just turn your iPhone sideways and it switches to give you a wider view." I'd tell you short, sweet, and right to the point, just like that. So that's what we do throughout the book. It's not a "tell-me-all-about-it" book, instead it's a "show-me-how-to-do-it" book.

Before Reading This Book!

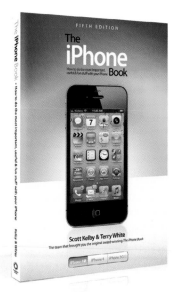

(4) There's a bonus video just for you. Terry and I shot a special video, and in it we give you some extra iPhone tips, show you some of our favorite accessories, and share some of the ways we use our iPhones, so once you're done reading the book, take a minute and check it out at **http://kelbytrain-ing.com/books/iphone4S**. By the way, those that skip over this quick intro will never even know it's there. Plus, they'll all start with Chapter 1, even if this is their second or third iPhone, so it serves 'em right, eh?

(5) The intro page at the beginning of each chapter is designed to give you a quick mental break, and honestly, they have little to do with the chapter. In fact, they have little to do with anything, but writing these off-the-wall chapter intros is kind of a tradition of mine (I do this in all my books), but if you're one of those really "serious" types, you can skip them because they'll just get on your nerves.

(6) There's also a bonus tips chapter in the book. Although we put lots of cool tips (we call 'em "iTips") throughout the book, you can never have enough tips (stuff like little-known shortcuts, suggestions, or tricks that can make using your iPhone easier or more fun), so in this fifth edition of the book, there's a special bonus chapter of nothing but "killer" tips (Chapter 14).

(7) If your iPhone's screen doesn't look like what you see here, then you haven't updated your iPhone with the free iOS 5 software from Apple. So, just connect your iPhone to your computer, launch Apple's iTunes, and when you do, you'll get a dialog telling you about the new software. Just click Download and Install, and then everything will look like what you see here in the book. Okay, that's it—you're ready to roll!

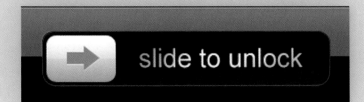

Chapter One

The Bare Essentials

10 Things Brand New iPhone Users Need to Know

If you've already been using your iPhone for a few weeks, skip right to Chapter 2

It's a tradition of mine to name my chapters after movie, TV show, or song titles, so I was originally going to name this chapter *Basic Training* after the 1985 movie by the same name (or the 1971 version of *Basic Training*, or the 2006 version, which went straight to video despite the fact it starred The Rock). But I started to wonder how many people would actually read a chapter that has the word "basic" in the title. It's sad, but nobody really wants to learn the basics anymore—they want to jump into the deep end of the pool and start with some advanced techniques, because they figure the basic stuff is too basic for them. So basically, I thought instead about using the title from the movie *Basic Instinct*. Now, I never actually saw the movie myself (didn't it have Scatman Crothers in it?), but I heard it was better than *Basic Instinct 2*, which I think starred Carrot Top and Ernest Borgnine (but since I didn't see that one either, I can't swear they were actually in it). So I started thinking of a term that meant basics but didn't have the downside of the word basics, and I came up with "essentials." Because this chapter covers the essential stuff you'll need to really make the most of your iPhone, but "essentials" has no marketing flair. No pizzaz. No bling. (No bling?) So I thought, what device do American marketers use to capture the attention of today's most coveted demographic (people with credit left on their Visa cards), and then *Bare Essentials* (from the short-lived 1991 TV series of the same name) came to mind. It sounds just naughty enough to trick someone into reading it, but not so naughty that Snoop Dogg would read it. That brings up an interesting question. What are you doing here?

Turning Your iPhone On, Off, and Putting It to Sleep

To turn on your iPhone, press-and-hold the **Sleep/Wake button** at the top (shown circled here in red on the left). After a moment, the Apple logo will appear, and then you'll get the Unlock screen. Press lightly on the arrow button, and slide it to the right to get to the Home screen, which is your main jumping off point to all the different things the iPhone can do. To turn your iPhone completely off, press-and-hold the Sleep/Wake button for around four seconds and a red **Slide to Power Off button** will appear (shown above right). Press lightly on it and slide it to the right. Your screen will turn black, you'll see a small round status icon for just a moment, then your iPhone will power off. To save battery life when you're not using the iPhone, press the **Sleep/Wake button** once to put it to sleep—you'll hear a little click sound, then your screen will go black (don't worry—it will still receive calls and text messages). To wake it from sleep, either tap that button again, or press the Home button (the round "real" button just below the screen). By the way, if you're not doing anything on your iPhone, in about 45 seconds, it dims the brightness of the screen (to save battery), and then about 15 seconds later, if you still haven't done anything, it puts itself to sleep.

---

iTip: Canceling the Shutdown

*If you get to the "power down" screen and then decide you didn't want to actually turn off your iPhone after all, just tap the **Cancel button** and it will go back to the screen you were on. If you do nothing for about 30 seconds, that will also cancel the shutdown.*

Using Your iPhone's Touchscreen

The touchscreen on your iPhone works amazingly well, and there are just a few little things to learn to make the most of it. Here are the three biggies:

(1) You don't have to press hard. It just takes a light tap on the touchscreen to launch an app (short for application), to choose any button, or select anything. It's surprisingly sensitive, which is great.

(2) You can zoom in much closer on part of a webpage, or email message, or photo, etc., by either: (a) double-tapping on the area you want to zoom in on, or (b) "pinching out," which is where you pinch your index finger and thumb together, then touch the screen with them pinched together, and then spread them apart. As you spread out your fingers, the screen zooms in. To zoom back out, start with your fingers apart—touch the top of the screen with your index finger and the bottom with your thumb—and pinch inward until they touch (like you're trying to pinch the screen).

(3) To scroll, or move something (like a slider), you touch the screen lightly and just "swipe" from left to right across the screen (Apple calls this "flicking," but it feels more like a swipe to me). For example, to see the album art in your iPhone's Music app, just touch an album lightly with your finger and kind of flick it (like you're flipping pages in a book). To scroll or move faster, swipe faster.

Getting Back to the Home Screen

The Home screen is pretty much your starting off point for…well…everything. It's where all your apps are, and it's where you go first to do everything from making a call to playing a song, so you need a quick way to get there. So, how important is getting to the Home screen? Well, there's only one "hard" button (an actual real button you can feel) on the face of the iPhone (it's found just below the touchscreen), and its main job is to take you to the Home screen, no matter what else you're doing. Just press it once, and the Home screen appears (as seen above). Of course, if you press it more than once, other stuff happens, but we'll cover that later. For now, know that you're always just one click away from this Home screen.

Making Phone Calls

Start at the Home screen, then tap on Phone. To dial a number, tap the **Keypad button**, and a standard telephone keypad appears. Now, just dial the number you want (it even makes those tone dialing sounds when you dial the number), and tap the green Call button. To end a call, tap the red End button. If you make a mistake while dialing the number, tap the Back button (to the right of the Call button). Before you make the call, if you want to add the number of the person you're about to call to your contacts list (your address book, basically), then tap the button to the left of the Call button, and it brings up a menu where you can create a new contact for the person at this number, or add it to a contact you've already created (much more on this, and all the cool features of the iPhone's phone, are in Chapter 2). One more thing: If somebody calls you, trust me—without any further explanation, you'll know what to do (see above right).

---

iTip: Switching to Silent Mode

*If you want to switch your iPhone to Silent mode, just move the **Ring/Silent switch** (found on the top-left side of your iPhone) toward the back of the iPhone—you'll see a large icon appear onscreen. Switch back to regular Ring mode by moving the Ring/Silent switch back toward the screen side of your iPhone.*

Using Your iPhone's Built-In Speaker

TERRY WHITE

Just tap the **Speaker button** that appears onscreen while your call is in progress. When you tap that button, it will turn solid blue to let you know the speakerphone is active. To turn the speakerphone off, tap that solid blue button again.

iTip: Keeping Your iPhone Private

Want to keep the info on your iPhone private? Then password protect it, so each time it wakes from sleep it asks you to input your secret four-digit password. To learn how to do this, see Chapter 7.

How to Send Text Messages

Start at the Home screen, then tap Messages. The first time you send a text message, this will take you directly to the New Message screen, where you can type and send your text. After that, tapping Messages will take you to your Messages list. So, to send a text message from there, tap the button in the top-right corner of the screen (it looks like a page with a pencil on it). In the To field, enter the phone number (or just a name if they're already in your contacts list—more on your contacts list in Chapter 2), then tap once in the field to the right of the camera icon and type in your text. (Hey, what's the camera icon for? See Chapter 3 for more on that kind of stuff.) When you're done with your message, just tap the green **Send button** and your message is on its way (a little Sending status bar appears on the top of the screen, so you can see the progress of your message being sent). That's the bare bones basics on texting, but if you turn to Chapter 3, you'll find lots more cool stuff your iPhone can do.

iTip: If You Miss a Call or a Text Message

If your iPhone is asleep and you miss a text message or call, it keeps track of all this stuff in the Notification Center, which makes it easy for you to quickly see what you missed. To get to these alerts, just go to the top of your screen and swipe downward to see the Notification Center. In it, you'll see a list of what you missed, any calendar event, weather, and stocks. If you want to reply to a text, voicemail, etc., listed there, just tap on it and it takes you right to that app.

Using the Built-In Keyboard

Anytime you need to type something on your iPhone, a keyboard automatically appears onscreen. The keys are kind of small, but as you type, a large version of the letter you just typed pops up in front of your finger so you can see instantly if you hit the right letter. I can tell you from experience that the more you use this keyboard, the easier it gets, so if you wind up misspelling just about every word when you first start, don't sweat it—in just a couple of days, you'll be misspelling only every third or fourth word. There's also a pretty clever Auto-Correction function. Although it will suggest a word while you're typing it, go ahead and finish the word (especially if you've spelled it wrong) and it will replace your misspelled word with the correct word (95% of the time). You do have to get used to typing a word, seeing that you've misspelled it, and continuing to type. If you do that, you'll be amazed at how quickly you'll be able to type using this keyboard.

---

iTip: Fixing Your Typos

If you need to go back and fix a typo that the Auto-Correction feature didn't catch, just press-and-hold approximately where the typo occurred and a magnifying Loupe appears onscreen so you can not only clearly see the location of your cursor, but you can move the cursor with your finger, as well, to quickly let you fix the mistake.

Downloading Songs/Videos Right to Your iPhone

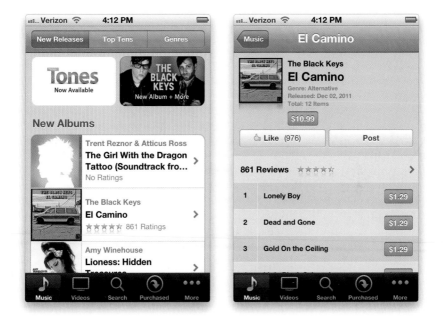

You can wirelessly download songs, TV shows, movies, podcasts, music videos, and more, using the iTunes app. It comes pre-installed on your iPhone, and you'll find it on the Home screen—just tap once on **iTunes** and it takes you to the iTunes Store. Once you're there, it's easy to find songs and videos to buy or rent, and then download directly to your iPhone (for more on using the iTunes Store, see Chapter 10, but for now, I just wanted to let you know that you can buy music and videos, right from your iPhone, without having to use your computer at all).

Flipping Your View

Because the iPhone is a phone, you probably wind up holding it vertically (tall), like you would any other phone, but the iPhone was the first phone to let you turn it on its side, automatically changing your view to widescreen. This is incredibly handy when watching movies (well, it's more than handy—it automatically plays movies in the wide view, so you'll want to turn your iPhone on its side for sure), but beyond that it makes the touch-screen keyboard larger, you can see more of webpages, your photos are larger, you can see more of your emails (you get the picture). Most apps support a wide view, so just give it a shot—turn your iPhone sideways and it immediately changes your view to widescreen. Sweet!

Charging Your iPhone

There are two ways to charge your iPhone: (1) the AC power adapter (one end plugs into the dock connector at the bottom of your iPhone using the white USB cable that came with it, and the other end plugs into a standard household outlet), or (2) your iPhone will also charge anytime it's connected to your computer (you use that same USB cable, but you pull off the power plug on the end to reveal a standard USB plug. So, one end plugs into the dock connector on the bottom of your iPhone, and the other end plugs into the USB port on your computer). When your iPhone is charging, the little battery icon at the top right of the screen will display a lightning bolt icon on it. When the battery is fully charged, it will change into a power plug icon, instead. Apple also sells a charging dock, which is convenient because you just sit your iPhone in the Dock and it starts charging immediately (no plugging and unplugging), plus it stands your iPhone upright while it's charging (so you don't have to just lay it on a table), and it also has an audio plug in the back, which makes it easy to connect your iPhone to speakers or a stereo receiver. (*Note:* There are other ways to charge it, like car chargers, but you have to buy those separately.)

---
iTip: Charging Via Your Computer

While you can charge your iPhone directly from the USB port on your computer, the battery may drain, not charge, when the computer goes to sleep or is in hibernation mode. You also may not get enough power if you connect your iPhone to a USB hub— it's usually best to connect it directly to your computer's built-in USB port.

Chapter Two
Phoneheads
How to Use the Phone

 I thought "Phoneheads" was a great name for this chapter, but it's not the name of a song; it's the name of a band that plays electronic music, which is why you probably haven't heard of them. My guess is that you don't listen to much electronic music. I'm not talking about music made with electronics (like electric guitars or synths), I'm talking about the kind of music you hear your teenagers playing, and you shake your head in disgust telling them, "That's not music!" Then one day, when you hear Van Halen's "Jamie's Cryin'" playing on your oldies station, you look in your rear view mirror and tell your kids, "Now that's music!" The sad thing is—you're right. That was music. And the stuff kids are listening to today is nothing more than an aural assault on everything we hold sacred about "real" music, which includes: white headbands, skinny ties, parachute pants, big hair, the hood of Whitesnake's car, inexpensive gas, and cassette tapes. Now *that* was music. I'm pretty safe in saying all this because you bought an iPhone, which means you must be pretty well off (or just incredibly loose with money), because iPhones aren't cheap. That means you're probably in your late 30s or early 40s, and you think that electronic music isn't music, so when I wrote that earlier, you were nodding your head. But, there is a second scenario: one in which you're young, and have rich parents, and they bought you an iPhone because they're loose with money. In that case, make sure you check out Phonehead's track "Syrinx (TGM Mix)." I love that song!

Importing Contacts from Your Computer

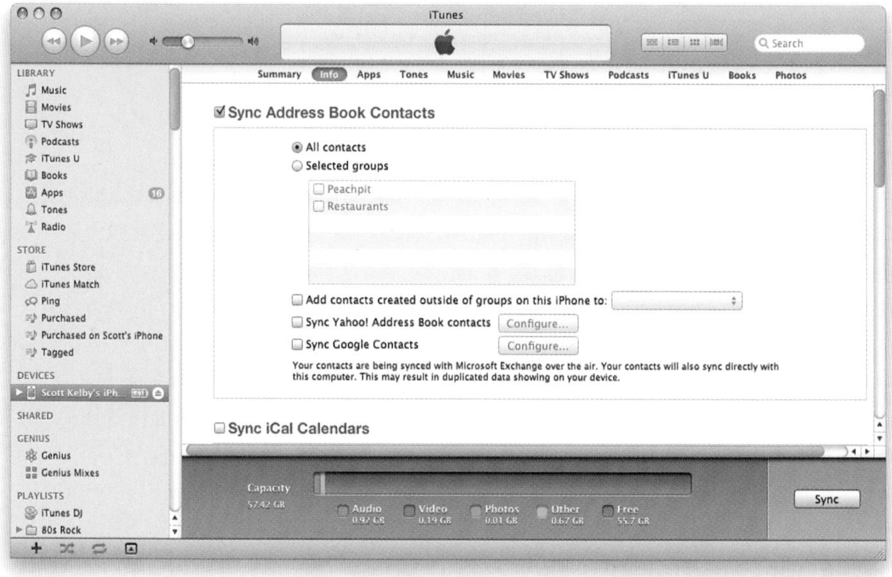

If you're a Mac user, you can import your contacts into your iPhone from four different contact managers. They are: (1) your Mac's Address Book application (2) Microsoft Outlook, (3) Yahoo! Address Book, or (4) Google Contacts. If your contacts are in any one of those four, when you plug your iPhone into your computer, it launches iTunes (shown above), and syncs the contacts on your computer with your iPhone (if you have this preference set). Or, you can click on the Info preferences tab in the main iTunes window, and choose which contacts you want to sync. If you're working on a corporate Microsoft Exchange Server, see your IT department, so they can give you the settings you'll need.

If you're a Windows PC user, it works pretty much the same way, but the four contact managers are: (1) Yahoo! Address Book, (2) Windows Contacts, (3) Microsoft Outlook, and (4) Google Contacts. Of course, if you're a corporate user on a Microsoft Exchange server, you can get your contacts over the air, as well. Again, see your IT department for the settings.

If you are getting contacts through your iCloud account, you can set your iPhone to sync through the iCloud settings in the Settings app. (See Chapter 9 for more on this.)

Importing Contacts from Your Old Phone

The first step is to transfer the contacts from your old phone onto your computer. Then you can go back to the previous page and follow those instructions to get those contacts from your computer to your iPhone. If your old phone doesn't automatically sync with your computer, you can use a utility called The Missing Sync by Mark/Space (www.markspace .com). Again, once you get your contacts on your computer, then follow the instructions on the previous page.

Making a Call by Dialing

If you want to dial a number, tap on the Phone app, then tap on the **Keypad button** to bring up the dialing buttons you see above. To dial a number, just tap the number keys. If you make a mistake, press the Back button (the button to the right of the green Call button) to erase that digit. Once you've dialed the correct number, tap the **Call button**.

---

iTip: Redialing a Number

*If you want to redial the last number you manually dialed, in the Phone app, tap the Keypad button and then tap **Call**. This will display the last number you dialed manually and tapping Call again will actually dial it.*

Saving a Dialed Number as a Contact

If you've just dialed a number using the keypad, and you want to add it as a contact (so you don't have to dial it again in the future), tap the **Add Contact button** (which appears to the immediate left of the green Call button). This brings up a menu where you can either create a new contact for this number, or add this number to an existing contact in your contacts list.

Turn a Recent Caller into a Contact

If someone calls you that isn't in your contacts list (but you'd like to add them), tap on the Phone app, then tap on Recents. Go to the number of the person you want to add as a contact, then tap on the button with the arrow in the blue circle to the right of their number. This brings up an Info screen, and near the bottom of this screen, tap the **Create New Contact button**. The New Contact screen appears with their number already entered—you just have to type in their name, address, etc. When you're done, tap the Done button in the upper-right corner of the screen.

---

iTip: Adding a Note to a Contact

*If you'd like to add a note to a contact (like a description of who the person is, or how you know them), tap on the contact, and when their Info screen appears, tap on the Edit button (in the top-right corner). Then, in the Info edit screen, scroll down and tap on Add Field, then scroll down and tap on **Notes** to add a Notes field, where you can type in your note using the keyboard that appears at the bottom of the screen.*

Dialing Someone in Your Contacts List

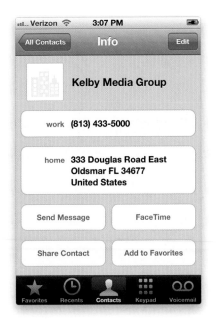

Tap on the Phone app, then tap on the **Contacts button** (okay, that was pretty obvious), and then tap on the person's name in the list. This brings up their full contact info, including a list of all their phone numbers you have added (cell number, home, office, etc.). To dial one of those numbers, just tap once on it and it starts dialing.

iTip: Jumping Right to a Letter

When you're in the All Contacts list, if you want to jump directly to a particular letter quickly, just tap once on the letter in the alphabetic list on the far-right side of the screen. You can also tap, hold, and slide up/down the list, as well.

Putting a Call on Hold to Call Someone Else

If you're on a call and need to make another one, you can put that call on hold and make a different call (kind of like having a two-line phone). On an iPhone 4 or 4S, just tap-and-hold the Mute button on the touchscreen (on an iPhone 3GS, tap the Hold button), then tap the **Add Call button**. This brings up your contacts list, where you can tap on a name to dial that contact (or, of course, you can just dial a number by tapping on the Keypad button that appears in the bottom-right corner of the All Contacts screen). If you want to switch back to your original call, you can just tap the Swap button or tap the call at the top of the screen. *Note:* This may be an optional service in some areas, depending on your carrier.

---

iTip: Muting a Phone Call and Using the Speakerphone

*If you're on a call and don't want the caller to hear what you're saying for a moment, tap the **Mute button** on the touchscreen. When you're ready to start talking again, tap the Mute button again. If you have a call in progress and want to hear your conversation through the iPhone's speaker, tap the **Speaker button** on the touchscreen.*

Making Instant Conference Calls

To add another person to the call you're on (for a three-way call), just tap the Add Call button on the touchscreen, and it brings up your contacts list. Tap the contact's name you want added to your three-way call, then tap their number, and it dials them. Now tap the **Merge Calls button** to add them to your conversation. If the person you want added to your call isn't in your contacts list, then you can dial them by tapping on the Keypad button in the bottom-right corner of the All Contacts screen.

---

iTip: Dialing an Extension

*So, let's say you dial a number and you get one of those "If you know your party's exten-sion, please dial it now" greetings. I know—how hard could it be? Actually, it's easy—if you know how. All you have to do is tap the **Keypad button** on your touchscreen, and then dial the extension. I know, it sounds really easy now, but I've seen people totally stumped when it happens to them.*

Pausing the Music to Take a Call

If you've got your headset (earbuds) on and you're listening to music and a phone call comes in, you can pause the song and jump over to take the call all in one click (that's right—it's a click, not a tap). There's a little button attached to the headset (about 5" from the right earbud itself. It doesn't look like a button, it looks like a thin little plastic rectangle). Click that button, and the song playing is paused, and it answers your call. When you're done with the call, click the button again to hang up and pick up the song right where you left off.

Check Your Email While You're On the Phone

If you're in a really boring phone conversation, and you want to do what everybody else in the world does—check your email—it makes things easier if you start by tapping the Speaker button (so you can still hear your conversation while you're looking at the touch-screen). Then, press the Home button, and tap **Mail**. Don't worry—your call will stay live even though you're doing something completely different. To return to your call screen, just tap once at the very top of your screen (where it says Touch to Return to Call), and it takes you back there. *Note:* Checking your email or surfing the Web while on the phone is not supported over most EDGE networks. It also only works on iPhones on AT&T's network—it is not currently supported on Verizon's or Sprint's networks (hey, don't shoot the messenger).

How to Know If You Missed Any Calls

If you miss a call while your iPhone is asleep, when you wake it, you'll see a list of any missed calls right on the Lock screen. If you tap the icon and swipe it to the right, it will return the call. You can also see all missed calls in your iPhone's Notification Center (you can see it by simply swiping downward from the top of any screen). In fact, you'll see a list of any callers (well, you'll see their name if they're in your contacts list. If they're not, you'll just see their number and Missed Call), and if they left a voicemail, you see that listed (rather than just Missed Call), too. If you tap on a missed call, it calls that person back. If you tap on a voicemail, it takes you to that voicemail message and starts playing it. If you skip the Notification Center, then you'll see that the icon for your Phone app now has a small red circle on its top-right corner with the total number of calls you either missed or that left you a voicemail. To see those calls, tap the Phone app, then tap Recents (to see your missed calls) or tap Voicemail (to see who left you a voicemail), but you can do all that with just one downward swipe to bring up the Notification Center (it saves you time and extra taps).

Returning Missed Calls

Tap on the Phone app, then tap the **Recents button** at the bottom of the screen. This brings up a list of all recent calls, and the calls you see listed in red are your missed calls. To see only your missed calls, tap the Missed button at the top. To return a missed call, just tap on it and it dials that number. (*Note*: The number of missed calls appears in a small red circle in the top-right corner of the Recents button.) If you get a call from an unfamiliar area code and number, it lists the city and state the call came from right below the number. Again, you can also return missed calls from the Notification Center by just swiping downward from the top of any screen and then tapping once on the missed call you want to return.

---

iTip: Clearing Recent Calls as a Group or Individually

*To clear all missed calls and your list of recent calls, in the Phone app, tap on Recents, tap the All button, then tap the Edit button, and a Clear button will appear in the top-left corner. Now, tap that **Clear button** and all recent and missed calls are removed. If you want to remove an individual call (missed or recent), swipe your finger to the left across the call you want to delete and a red Delete button will appear on the right side of the call listing. Tap that button to delete just that call. If you make a mistake and mark the wrong call to delete, just swipe back to the right.*

Seeing If You Have Voicemail Messages

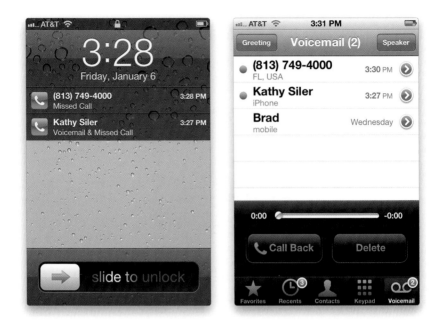

If a caller left you a voicemail message, you'll see the caller's name (if they're in your contacts list—if not, their phone number) onscreen when you wake your iPhone from sleep or in the Notification Center when you swipe downward from the top of any screen. When you tap the green Phone app, you'll see the Voicemail button, and on it you'll see a red circle displaying the number of messages you have waiting. To see a list of your voicemails (yes, you see a list—that's why Apple calls this "Visual Voicemail"), tap on the **Voicemail button**, and you'll see a list of the contacts (or numbers) who've left you a voicemail message, and when they called. Messages with a blue dot before them haven't been listened to yet.

Listening To and Deleting Voicemail Messages

The beauty of this system is you don't have to listen to your messages in order—you can tap directly on the message you want to hear and that message plays. To hear your messages through your iPhone's speaker, tap the Speaker button on the top right. You'll see a status bar that moves from left to right as your message plays, which shows you how long the message is. Now, here's the thing: When a message is new, you just tap on it and it plays. But once you've heard it, when you tap on the message, a little blue **Play/Pause button** appears before it. To hear the message again, tap that little blue button. To pause the message, tap that same little blue button again. To return a call, tap on the message, then tap the green **Call Back button**. To delete a message, tap on it, then tap on the red **Delete button**. Once you delete a message, it's not really deleted from your iPhone—it just moves that message to a deleted area (kind of the way deleting a file on your computer just puts it in your Trash or Recycle Bin). You can still see, and hear, your deleted messages by tapping on (I know—it's pretty obvious) Deleted Messages (at the end of your voicemail list). Once there, to move a deleted message back to your regular list, just tap on it, then tap the gray Undelete button. However, if you really want all of your deleted voicemails off your iPhone for good, once you're in the Deleted screen, just tap the Clear All button. Of course, you can also play the message from the Notification Center (just swipe downward from the top of any screen to make it appear). Here, you'll see a list of any recent voicemails. To hear a voicemail, just tap on the person's name in the list (or their number), and it takes you to the Voicemail screen you see above, and automatically plays their voicemail.

Replay Just Part of a Voicemail Message

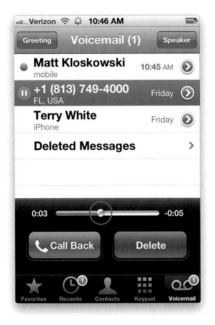

While your message is playing, you can grab the little slider and "scrub" back a few seconds and hear anything you just missed—in real time. So, for example, let's say you're listening to a message and the person on the message gives you a phone number. To hear that phone number again (without having to listen to the entire message again), you can just tap-and-hold on the little **status bar knob** and drag it back a little bit (just like you would scrub through a video), and hear it again.

Recording Your Outgoing Voicemail Message

By default, you get a generic "I'm not here, man" voicemail message, but creating your own custom message is really easy. Just tap on the Voicemail button, then in the top-left corner of the Voicemail screen, tap on the **Greeting button** to bring up the Greeting screen. You'll see two choices: (a) Default (the generic pre-recorded greeting), and (b) Custom (where you create your own). Tap on Custom, and Play and Record buttons appear at the bottom of the screen. Tap the white Record button, hold the iPhone up to your ear, and just say your message into it. When you're done, tap the red Stop button, and to hear it, tap the blue Play button. If you don't like your message, just tap the white Record button again and record a new message. When it sounds good to you, tap the Save button in the upper-right corner of the screen.

---

iTip: Singing Your Message

Don't sing messages into your iPhone, as a sensor was designed by Apple to detect really bad singing and when it analyzes your voice and determines that it is indeed bad singing, it automatically forwards your message, along with a picture of you, to YouTube where it's then featured in a public humiliation forum. Well, at least that's what I've been told.

Setting Up Call Forwarding

Tap on the Settings app, then in the Settings screen, tap on Phone. In the Phone settings screen, tap on **Call Forwarding** and you'll see an ON/OFF button (by default, it's off). To turn it on, tap this button. Now, you're probably wondering where your call is forwarded to. Once you turn on the Call Forwarding feature, if you don't already have a Forwarding To number entered, you'll see a screen where you enter that phone number. Now, this next part throws a lot of people: there's no OK or Save button. You just have to tap the Call Forwarding button in the top-left corner and it returns you to the main Call Forwarding screen, where you'll see the number you just added and the ON setting. When you want to turn the Call Forwarding feature off, go back to the same screen, and tap the ON button, and it will change to OFF. (*Note:* This applies to AT&T's network. Other networks may require you to make the changes online, with a link under the network's services in the Phone settings.)

Your iPhone's Version of Speed Dial

Your iPhone's name for speed dial is "Favorites," and to turn one of your contacts into a Favorite, just tap on their name in your contacts list to view the screen with their full contact info. Then, in the bottom-right corner of their Info screen, tap on the **Add to Favorites button** (shown circled here in red), and then choose whether to add that contact as a Voice Call or FaceTime favorite. Now, there is another way to do it, and that is to start at the Favorites screen (in the Phone app, tap the Favorites button), then tap the little **+ (plus sign) button** in the upper-right corner. This brings up your contacts list, and you just tap on the name of the contact you want added to your Favorites. If your contact has only one phone number (like just a home number, or just a cell number), then you'll just have to choose whether to add them as a Voice Call or FaceTime favorite, and they're immediately added as a Favorite. If they have multiple numbers, then it brings up all their numbers and you just tap on the number you want added as a Favorite.

Removing and Reordering Your Favorites

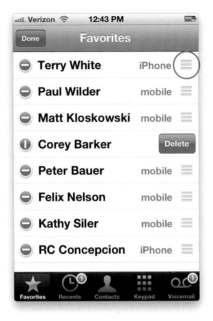

Tap the Edit button in the top-left corner of the Favorites screen, and a red circle with a – (minus sign) will appear before each Favorite. To remove a Favorite from your list, just tap directly on its red minus button, and a red Delete button will appear to its right (as seen above). Tap that **Delete button** and it's gone! To reorder them, tap on the Edit button, and then on the far right of each contact, just past the type of phone number (mobile, home, etc.), you'll see **three short horizontal lines** (circled in red above). Now, you're going to drag your contacts into the order you want them by tapping-and-holding on those lines and dragging your contact up or down (it's easier than it sounds).

Seeing the Contact Info for a Favorite

The Favorites screen is great because you can just tap the name of the contact you want to dial and the iPhone immediately begins calling that contact. However, sometimes the contact may have multiple phone numbers, such as home, work, mobile, etc., and you may not want to put every number in as a Favorite. So, the next time you need to dial a number for a Favorite contact that's not actually saved as a Favorite, bring up your Favorites list and then tap the **blue arrow button** next to the contact's name and the full Info screen appears for that contact with all the other numbers you have for them. From there, tap any one of those numbers to dial it.

Adding a Pause

If you're calling a number and you need to enter an extension (account number, PIN, etc.), you can add those pauses and additional numbers directly to your contact's Info screen. Tap on the Phone app, then tap on Contacts to bring up your contacts list. Tap on the contact that needs the additional string of numbers and pauses. Tap the Edit button in the top right of the screen, tap on the phone number that you need to edit, and tap the symbol key (+*#) at the bottom left of the keyboard. This will change the 4 key to a Pause key. Now you can tap the **Pause key** to enter a two-second pause, and then type the next string of numbers. If you need a longer pause, just continue to tap the Pause key for as many two-second pauses as you need. You can also add a hard pause by tapping the **Wait key**. This causes the iPhone to pause and wait until you tap the Dial button to send the numbers. Once you're done, tap Done at the top right of the screen to save the number and the contact's changes.

Adding New Contacts from Scratch

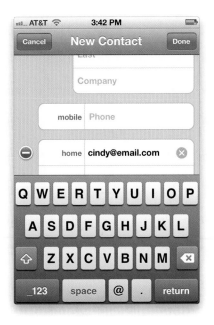

If you want to create a new contact from scratch, tap on the Phone app, then tap on the Contacts button, and tap the **+ (plus sign) button** in the upper-right-hand corner to bring up a New Contact screen. Tap on the info you want to add. For example, to add your new contact's email address, just tap on Home Email and you can then type in their email address using the keyboard at the bottom of the screen (you can also change Home to Work or Other by tapping on it and choosing a new label in the list that pops up). When you're done adding the email address, scroll up and down and add more info the same way. When you're finished adding the new contact info, tap the Done button in the top-right corner.

---

iTip: Getting Back to the Previous Screen

Here's a tip to help you think like your iPhone: most of the time, if you see a button in the upper-left corner of the screen, it acts like a Back button in a Web browser—pressing it will take you back to the previous screen you were on.

The Advantage of Contact Groups

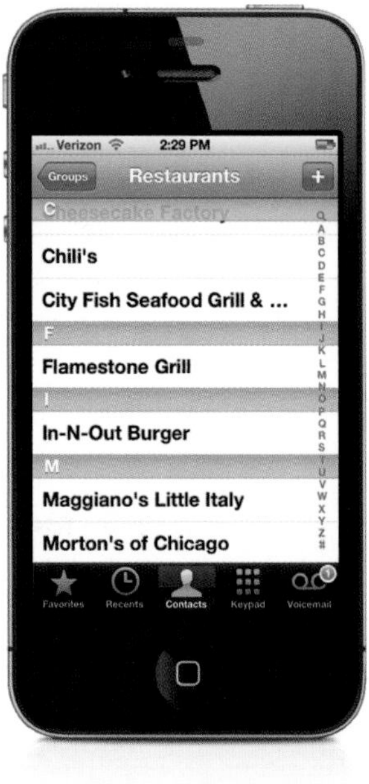

If the contact manager on your computer allows you to have caller groups, you can add them to your iPhone and it can make getting to the contacts you want much easier. For example, you could have a group for your favorite restaurants, and one just for your friends, and one for your co-workers, and…well, you get the idea. That way, when you tap on the Phone app, then tap on Contacts, you can tap the **Groups button** (in the upper-left corner) to see a list of your different groups. Then, you can tap on a group and see just those contacts (like seeing just your favorite restaurants, as shown above).

Seeing a Contact's Photo When They Call

Tap on the Phone app, then the Contacts button. Scroll to the contact you want to assign a photo to, tap their name, then tap the Edit button in the top-right corner of the screen. In the upper-left corner of the Info screen, tap on Add Photo. This brings up two buttons: **Take Photo** (so you can take a photo of your contact using your iPhone's camera), and **Choose Photo** (which lets you choose any photo you've already taken with or imported into your iPhone). If you tap the Choose Photo button, it takes you to your Photos screen, where you can find the photo you want and tap on it to assign to your contact. You'll get a screen where you can choose the size and position of the photo that will display when your contact calls (use your finger to slide it around, which basically crops the photo, or "pinch it" with your fingers to scale it up or down). When it looks good to you, tap the gray Choose button and you're done. If, instead, you tap the Take Photo button, just take the photo, scale and move it, and tap Use Photo. This is cool, but the picture won't be in the Camera Roll for download later. So if it's a picture you will want to use for something else, take the picture first and add it to the contact afterwards.

Shooting a Photo and Adding It to a Contact

If you want to take a photo using your iPhone's camera and then add it to an existing contact, tap on the Camera app. Aim the camera and take a photo of your contact by tapping the camera shutter button at the bottom center of the screen (or press the Volume Up button on the side of your iPhone). You'll hear the shutter sound to let you know the photo has been taken. To see the photo you just took, just swipe to the right. Tap on the photo, and a row of buttons appears along the bottom of the screen. Tap the button that looks like a box with an arrow coming out of it and a menu will pop up. To assign this photo to a contact, tap the **Assign to Contact button**, and it brings up your contacts list. Tap on the contact you want to assign that photo to, and it shows you how the final photo is going to look when the contact calls, so you can move and scale it the way you want (using your finger to slide the photo around onscreen, which basically crops the photo, or "pinching it" with your fingers to scale it up or down). When it looks good to you, press the gray Set Photo button and you're done.

Control the Size of Your Caller ID Photos

If you've added photos to your contacts, you may have noticed that some of them display full screen and some only display in the upper-right corner of the screen when a contact calls. This all boils down to how the photo was added to the contact. If you added the photo from your computer's address book, then it will likely display the photo small in the upper-right corner of the screen. However, if you added the photo directly on your iPhone, either using the iPhone's camera or from photos in your iPhone's Photo Library, they will display full screen when the contact calls.

---

iTip: Seeing Two Names on Your Caller ID

You may have noticed that your caller ID display will sometimes show two names. This happens when you have two contacts in your iPhone with the same number (mine says "Carla or Terry White" when my wife calls from home). The iPhone doesn't choose sides— it just displays both names when a call comes in from that number.

Search for a Contact

When you go to your contacts list (from the Phone app or the Contacts app), there will be a **search field** at the top of the list. Tap in it to get the keyboard, start typing the name of the contact you're looking for, and the iPhone will immediately begin narrowing down the list to names that match what you've typed. Once you see the name you're looking for, you can stop typing and tap the contact you found to bring up their Info screen. You can also do a system-wide search using the **Spotlight feature** by either pressing the Home button from the first Home screen or by swiping to the right from your first Home screen.

---

iTip: Narrowing Down Your Search

If you want to narrow the list down even further, type the first letter of the first name, then type a space, and then type the first letter of the last name. This will narrow the list down to only the contacts with those initials. You can still keep typing to get to the name you want. So if you wanted to find Scott Kelby, you'd type "S Kel" and that would narrow the list down quicker than having to scroll through multiple Scotts.

Turning the Ringer Off

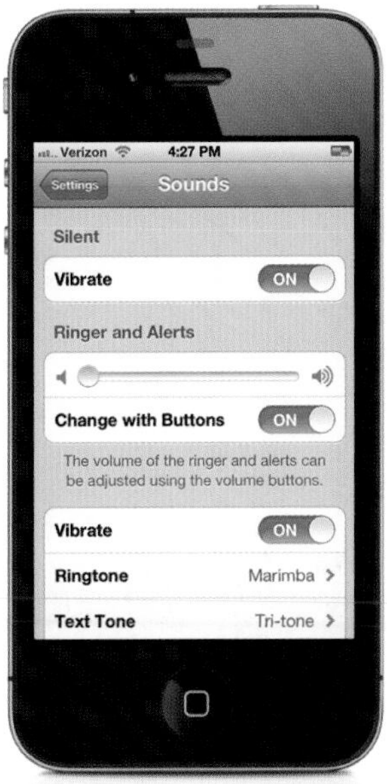

If you don't want to hear your iPhone's ringer at all, tap on the Settings app. In the Settings screen, tap on Sounds, then in the Ringer and Alerts section, tap-and-drag the **volume slider** all the way to the left. This turns your ring volume off. Your phone will still vibrate when a call comes in, but there won't be an audible ring. If you want to turn that vibration off, as well, just above Ringtone, turn Vibrate off by tapping on its **ON/OFF button**. You can also turn the ringer off by moving the **Ring/Silent switch** (found on the top-left side of the iPhone) toward the back of the iPhone to Silent mode.

---

iTip: Stop the Ringing

*If a call comes in, and you can't take it right then, but don't want the phone to continue ring-ing, then just press the **Sleep/Wake button** on the top of the iPhone. This stops the ringing and sends the call into your voicemail.*

Choosing Your Ringtone

The default ringtone for your iPhone is a marimba sound, but if you'd like to change it, tap on the Settings app. In the Settings screen, tap on Sounds, then in the Ringer and Alerts section, tap on **Ringtone**, and it takes you to a screen listing all the built-in ringtones and any custom ringtones you've synced to your iPhone. You'll see a checkmark to the right of Marimba, telling you that it's the current ringtone. To change it, tap on the name of the one you want. That ringtone plays (so you can hear if you really want to select it), and if you want to keep this new sound as your ringtone, just leave that screen (tap the Sounds button in the top-left corner of the Ringtone screen, or press the Home button).

Assigning Ringtones to Specific Callers

If you'd like to assign a specific ringtone to a contact (for example, I have a ringtone assigned to my wife's cell phone number, so I instantly know it's her without even looking at my phone), here's what to do: Tap on the Phone app, then tap the Contacts button. Tap on the contact you want to assign a ringtone to, then when their Info screen appears, tap the Edit button in the top right, then tap on Default (next to Ringtone), and you'll be taken to the Ringtone screen. To assign a ringtone to this contact, just tap on one (it will play a sample of the ringtone when you tap on it). When you find the one you want, just tap the Save button at the top right of the screen, and it returns you to the contact's Info screen, where you'll see the name of the ringtone you just assigned in the Ringtone field. Tap the Done button, and now when this contact calls, you'll hear their custom ringtone rather than the default ringtone that you'll hear when anyone else calls.

Stop People You Call from Seeing Your Number

If you want to call somebody, but you'd prefer that they not see your number, tap on the Settings app. Scroll down and tap on Phone, and in the Phone settings screen, you'll see **Show My Caller ID**. Tap on that control to bring up the Show My Caller ID screen with an ON/OFF button. Just tap that button to switch this feature off. (*Note:* This applies to AT&T's network. Other networks may require you to make the changes online, with a link under the network's services in the Phone settings.)

Headsets or Bluetooth in Your Car

If you have a Bluetooth wireless headset, or you want to pair your iPhone to your car's Bluetooth feature, here's what to do: First you have to put your headset (or your car's Bluetooth feature) in Discoverable mode, which means you put it in a mode where other Bluetooth devices can find it. How this is done is different for every headset or car make and model, so look at your headset's instruction manual (or your car's owner's manual) for how to make it "discoverable." Once it's discoverable, tap on the Settings app, then tap on General, and tap on **Bluetooth**. When the Bluetooth screen appears, tap the ON/OFF button to turn the Bluetooth feature on. This starts your iPhone searching for any discoverable Bluetooth devices (like your wireless headset or your car's Bluetooth feature) that are within about 30 feet of where you are. Once it finds a Bluetooth device, it displays that device's name. Tap the Not Paired button, which will bring up a screen where you enter the PIN for your device (check the instructions that come with your headset or car kit for how to find this information), then tap Pair, and they'll be paired (luckily, you only have to go through this process the first time. After that, it automatically recognizes your headset, or car).

Set Up to Make FaceTime Video Calls

To make a FaceTime video call, first you need to make sure both people on the call have an iPhone 4 or 4S (you can't make video calls with an iPhone 3GS, because it doesn't have a camera on the front of it) or a Mac or another iOS device that supports FaceTime. You also need to be on a Wi-Fi network (so, for me, this means I can make FaceTime calls any time I'm at the office, or at home, or at a Wi-Fi hotspot). If you've got both of these covered, then you'll just need to turn the FaceTime feature on (you only have to do this once). Tap on the Settings app, scroll down and tap on FaceTime, and then turn **Face-Time** on by tapping the ON/OFF button. Now your iPhone is all set to make FaceTime video calls. By the way, since FaceTime is essentially an Internet video call, it doesn't use up your cellular phone minutes. (How cool is that?)

Making a FaceTime Video Call

Now that you've got your iPhone set up to make FaceTime video calls, there are four different ways to make one:

(1) Tap on the Phone app, and then tap on Contacts to find the person you want to have a FaceTime video call with. When you get to their Info screen, tap the **FaceTime button** (as shown circled above left). If you have more than one phone number or email address for this person (like home, mobile, etc.), it will bring up a list of them. Just tap the one you want (remember to call their iOS device), and it makes the FaceTime call.

(2) You can make a regular phone call using the Phone app, and once the person answers, you can tap the **FaceTime button** (shown circled above right) to switch to a video call.

(3) If you recently had a FaceTime video call with someone, if you tap on the Phone app, then tap the **Recents button**, you'll see their name (or number) on this screen, along with a video camera icon. If you tap on their name to call them, it redials as a FaceTime call.

(4) If you want to have a FaceTime video call with someone who doesn't have an iPhone (they have an iPad 2, or an iPod touch), then you'll need to choose their FaceTime email address instead to start the FaceTime call.

Whichever method you choose, the person you're calling will have to accept your FaceTime call invitation. Once they tap **Accept**, your video call begins.

During Your FaceTime Call

The camera on the front of the phone turns on first to show you a preview of how you'll look to the person on the other end. Once they accept your call, your image shrinks down to a small thumbnail up in the top-right corner of your screen (like a TV picture-in-picture view), and their video image fills your screen. You talk just like you're using the speaker-phone feature. If you need to pause the video part of your call (but keep the speakerphone live), press the Home button (this is handy if you need to look up something in another app). To return to video, tap the green bar at the top. To mute your mic, press the Mute icon in the bottom left. Normally, the person you're having a FaceTime call with will see you during the call, but if you want, you can switch to the camera on the back of your iPhone, so they see whatever you point your camera at, by tapping the Camera Swap icon in the bottom-right corner (the camera with the circular arrow around it). The tiny thumbnail in the top-right corner now shows the camera's view on the back of your iPhone, so you can see what they're seeing. Also, just rotate your iPhone sideways to get a wider shot. To switch back, press the same Camera Swap icon. To end the call, tap the End button.

iTip: You Can Move the Tiny Thumbnail Preview Window

Once you start a FaceTime video call, what your camera is showing shrinks down to a small thumbnail preview in the upper-right corner. If it's blocking something you want to see, move it by pressing-and-holding on it, then dragging it to a different corner.

Use FaceTime and Not Cellular Minutes

One of the hidden treasures in the iPhone's FaceTime feature is that it only works over Wi-Fi. This means that since you and the person you're talking to each have an iPhone 4 or 4S (or another compatible iOS device) and are on a Wi-Fi network, you can make unlimited FaceTime calls without ever using any cellular minutes. This is great for international travel or any other situation where roaming would be expensive.

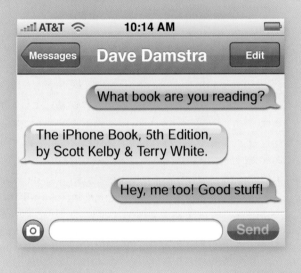

Chapter Three

Message in a Bottle

Sending Text Messages

"Message in a Bottle" (by The Sheriffs) is a better name than it first sounds, because there is nothing in your iPhone that says "Texting." Nope. Instead, you send texts using an app called Messages. Now, I now what you're thinking, "Wouldn't an app named Messages be where you go to check your voicemail messages?" Nope, that's called Voicemail (which is in the Phone app). So, couldn't they just have called the app "Texting" or "Text?" Sure. Could you just call The Police (who did "Message in a Bottle") The Sheriffs, since they pretty much do the same thing? Ahh, see, this is why this is all so sticky, but in the secret world of app naming, the person who names the app the furthest from what it actually does gets a huge bonus at the end of the year (along with a large trophy they hold above their head as they skate around the rink). Anyway, in this case, Messages isn't a bad name, because it's half of the phrase "Text Messages," so the person that named this app won't be skating around with the trophy anytime soon. Neither will the person who named the Stocks, Weather, Camera, Photos, Maps, Calendar, Mail, Phone, or Clock apps. In fact, I'm not sure if anybody at Apple will be up for the award this year, because it all makes too much sense. Ya know, Microsoft has their own Windows phone out now, but of course their corporate slogan is "Making simple everyday things just that much harder," and although I haven't actually used a Windows phone (in fact, I'm not sure really anyone has), I imagine their apps are named in a very Microsoft-like way. For example, I would guess that their texting app would probably be called something like "Bing XP," and their phone app would be something like "Excel Chart," and their calendar app would probably be called "Office Bing." Hey, I heard that the original name for the Windows phone was supposed to be "Zune iBing Vista Maintenance Pack 4a.10B."

Sending Text Messages

Tap on the Messages app, then tap on the button with a square with a pencil in it (in the upper-right corner of the screen), which brings up the New Message screen. At the top, you type your contact's name, and as soon as you start to type, it searches for the name in your contacts list. If they're not in your contacts list, just type in their phone number. Now, tap once in the field above the keyboard, type in your text message, then tap the green **Send button**. Your messages appear in green bubbles, replies will appear in gray bubbles, and visually it looks like you're having a conversation. If you're sending a text message to someone else who has an iPhone 4 or 4S, then your Send button and message will appear in blue (more on this feature, called "iMessage," on page 55).

Sending Messages to Multiple People

It's possible to send the same text or picture message to two or more people at once. Launch Messages and tap the button with a square with a pencil in it in the top right. Start typing in the name of the first person (or phone number, if they're not in your contacts list), and tap their name if it comes up in the search results below the To field (or if you typed in their phone number, tap in the message field, then tap back into the To field), then type in another name or number for another person you want to send the message to. You can also tap the + (plus sign) button to add contacts directly from your contacts list. Now, in the past, if you sent a message to two or more people, when they responded, each person's response would start a new one-on-one individual text thread between you and just that person. But, now, in iOS 5, if you have Group Messaging turned on in the Messages settings in the Settings app, when someone responds, they automatically respond to all the other recipients, as well—kind of like a group conversation.

Seeing If You Have Text Messages

When a text message comes in, the sender's name and the first line of their text message appear right at the top of your screen for a few seconds, as shown above left (of course, if you don't have their name in your contacts list, you'll only see their phone number and not their name). If your iPhone is asleep when their text message comes in, then when you wake it, you'll see their message on the Lock screen. If you have more than one new message, you can swipe downward to see all of them listed at the top of the Lock screen (shown above right), and to see the text of any message in the list, just unlock your phone. If you look at the Messages app icon on the Home screen, you'll see it keeps track of how many unread messages you have, by showing that number in a little red circle on the top-right corner of the icon (so, if you see a 4 in a red circle, that means you have four unread messages).

iTip: Seeing Which Text Messages Haven't Been Read Yet

If you see a number on the Messages app icon, tap on it, and the messages in the list with a blue dot beside them are the ones you haven't read yet.

iMessage: Send Unlimited Free Texts! Really!

iMessage is a very cool texting feature (built into the regular Messages app) that lets you send texts to other iOS 5 users (iPhone, iPad, iPod touch) via Wi-Fi or 3G, rather than using your phone's data plan, so you don't get charged standard messaging rates (in fact, you don't get charged at all, so think of this as free, unlimited texting). To turn on iMessage, tap the Settings app, then tap on Messages, and turn on iMessage (as shown above left). Now, you have free unlimited texting as long as: (a) you have a Wi-Fi or 3G connection *and* (b) you're sending your text to another device that is using iOS 5 or newer, and that has iMessage turned on, too. If your text is sent as an iMessage, two things happen: (1) you'll see the word iMessage with a horizontal line appear right above your text conversation (as shown circled above right), and (2) your text message will now appear in a blue talk bubble, rather than the usual green. To send iMessages to friends who are using an iPod touch or an iPad (any iOS 5 or newer device), you just need the email address they registered when they set up iMessage (and, of course, they need to have an Internet connection).

📶 iTip: Another iMessage Advantage Is You'll See When They Start Typing

When you text with iMessage, as soon as the person you're texting with starts to reply to your text, you'll see a little talk bubble with three little dots appear on their side of the conversation, letting you know that they're working on their response. You'll miss this when you're not using iMessage, because it's really amazingly handy.

How to Know If You're Sending an iMessage

One way to tell if the person you're about to text will receive your text as an iMessage (meaning, you're using free unlimited texting to this person) is to look at the color of the Send button for your text. If the button is blue, you're sending a free iMessage. If it's green, you're using regular texting (and you're paying. Well, you're probably paying— it just depends on your texting plan, but you know what I mean). Once you've started texting, another visual reminder is the color of your talk bubble. If you're using iMessage, it's blue. If not, it's green. Green means "Go!" as in "Go talk them into getting an iPhone, so your text messaging to them is free (it'll be free for them, too!)."

Deleting Individual Messages

If you want to delete an individual text message from your conversation, just tap the Edit button in the top-right corner of the message screen, then tap right on the text you want to delete. This adds a red checkmark beside the comment, letting you know that's the one you've marked to be deleted (if you want to delete other comments, tap on those, too). Now, just tap the red **Delete button** on the bottom left of the screen. If you change your mind, just tap on the text again.

---

iTip: Deleting Entire Conversations

*If you want to delete an entire text conversation (as if it never happened), go to that conversation, tap the Edit button up top, then tap the **Clear All button** that appears at the top left of the screen. There's also a shortcut: in your list of messages, just swipe sideways over the message, and a red **Delete button** will appear. Tap it, and it's gone.*

Forwarding Individual Messages

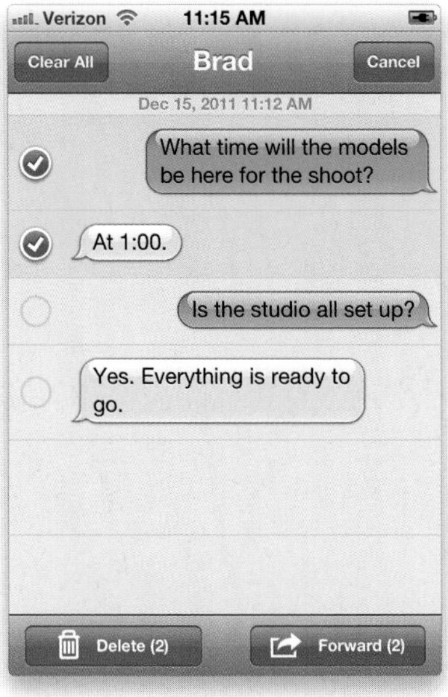

Tap on the Messages app and go to the particular message that you want to forward all or part of. Tap the **Edit button** in the upper-right corner of the screen and you'll see circles appear next to each response in the message. You can select one or more of them by tapping on their talk bubbles, and then you can forward them to someone else by tapping the Forward button at the bottom of the screen. This brings up a New Message screen with the responses you selected already in the message field. Just type in a contact or phone number to send it to, and tap Send.

iTip: Calling a Phone Number You've Been Texted

If someone texts you a phone number, you'll notice it's underlined in blue. That's because your iPhone recognizes that it's a phone number, and that blue underline means it's a "live link." So, if you tap on that number, it dials it for you. Sweet!

If Your Text Doesn't Go Through

You'll see a little red alert exclamation point appear to the right of the message (this will usually only happen if you're in an area with really bad cell reception). To have it try to resend the text message, just tap on the exclamation point icon, then tap the **Try Again button**. If it's successful, the message will appear in a bubble just like always and the exclamation point icon will be gone. Otherwise, it will stay there in the bubble with the red warning beside it. Also, if you tap the Send button, and then switch to another app (thinking your message was sent with no problem), the Messages app will try to alert you that the message didn't go by adding a red exclamation point warning to the Messages app's icon (as shown above right).

---

iTip: If Your iMessage Doesn't Go Through

If you send an iMessage, but it seems to have stalled (probably due to bad reception coverage), you can send the message via cellular text messaging by just tapping-and-holding on the message, and if it hasn't been delivered yet, you can choose to send it as a text message instead. Also, if the message does fail, you'll be given the choice to send it as a text message, or it will eventually just send it as one, but with this tip you don't have to wait for it to time out/fail.

Sending Photos or Videos in a Text Message

Go to Messages and tap the button with a square with a pencil in it in the top right. Now, type in the name or phone number of the person you're texting, then tap the **Attach Media button** to the left of the message field (the camera icon). A menu pops up asking if you want to take a photo or video or choose a photo already on your iPhone. If you tap Take Photo or Video, it takes you to the Camera app to take your photo (or video). Once you take it, you'll see a preview of it. If you don't like it, tap the Retake button to try again. If you like it, tap the Use button, and it attaches that photo to a text message (and it automatically compresses the size of it). If you tapped the Choose Existing button instead, it takes you to your photo albums, where you can choose a photo in any album by just tapping on it. It shows you a preview of the photo (or video), and if it looks good, tap the Choose button (if not, tap Cancel). It'll appear in a text bubble, and now just tap the Send button. Also, if you choose a photo to send, but before you send it, you change your mind, just hit the Backspace key (on the keyboard) a few times to delete it. If someone sends you a photo or video, it appears in a text bubble, too, just like text. To see it larger, just tap directly on the photo.

---

iTip: Turning On MMS Messaging

*If, for some reason, the ability to send MMS (photo and video) messages isn't turned on, tap the Settings app, then tap on Messages. Tap the **MMS Messaging ON/OFF button** to turn it on.*

Video Quality and Text (MMS) Messaging

Video files are much, much larger in file size than photos, so your iPhone has to greatly compress and shrink your video clip's physical size, so it's small enough to be delivered as an MMS message. Because of that, the quality of the video you're sending isn't quite as good as the original video you shot. It will probably look a little pixelated and generally a bit lower in quality than how it looked after you viewed it on your own iPhone. So, if keeping the original video quality intact is really important to you, then instead of sending the video as a text message, email it, and it will look a lot better.

---

iTip: Seeing More Messages

When you look at the list of text conversations you've had with a particular person, it only displays the last 50 texts between you two. So, if you need to find texts previous to those 50, from the top of the message list, tap on **Load Earlier Messages**, and it will load the next earlier batch.

Sending Voice Memos in a Text Message

If you've recorded a voice memo, you can send that in a text message. Start in the Voice Memos app (in the Utilities folder), then tap on the button to the right of the VU meter to see a list of your voice memos. Tap on the voice memo you want to send, then tap the blue Share button at the bottom left. A menu will pop up; tap **Message** and it attaches that voice memo to a new, blank text message. Now just type in the recipient's name (or phone number), and then tap the Send button. If you want to add any text along with your voice memo, just tap once on the message field, and type in your message.

---

iTip: Searching Through Your Text Messages

If there's a particular message you're trying to find, you can search by any word in the text. So, if you were talking about pizza delivery, you could search for the word "pizza" by using the **Search field** *at the top of the Messages screen.*

Use Siri to Do Your Texting for You

If you don't want to type your texts (maybe you're driving), then just let Siri type and send your texts for you. Say, "Send a text to [the person's name]," then Siri will ask you, "What do you want to say to [the person's name]?" Now, if Siri gets the name wrong or doesn't understand you, she will let you know and guess which of your contacts' names you said. If she's right, say, "Yes," and she will then ask you what you want to say. Just say your message (don't speak really fast, of course). When you're done, pause for a couple of seconds and Siri will show your message, and then ask if you're "ready to send it." Just say "Yes," and off it goes, all without you touching your keyboard. Learn more about Siri in Chapter 8.

Other Ways to Text Your Contacts

There are a couple of other places where you can directly text from, rather than having to go to the Home screen and tap Messages every time. For example, if you're looking at a contact in the Contacts app, you'll see a button there for **Send Message**. Tap it, choose the phone number or email to send it to, and it takes you to the New Message screen with that person's name already entered for you. If you want to text the person you're currently talking with on the phone (I use this to text the person a phone number we talked about, without them having to write it down), in the Phone app, tap on Contacts, tap on the person's name you're talking to, then tap the Send Message button. If you're looking at a Voicemail message instead, and want to text the person who left you the voice message, tap the **blue arrow button** to the right of the voice message, then tap the Send Message button.

---

iTip: Turning Off the Pop-Up Previews

If you'd rather not see the pop-up onscreen text message previews, tap on the Settings app, then tap Notifications. Under In Notification Center, tap on Messages, and turn off ***Show Preview***.

Turning Off the "You Got a Text Message" Sound

ıll.. AT&T	11:17 PM

Settings | **Sounds**

Change with Buttons | **ON**

The volume of the ringer and alerts can be adjusted using the volume buttons.

Vibrate | **ON**

Ringtone | Marimba >

Text Tone | None >

New Voicemail | Tri-tone >

New Mail | Ding >

Sent Mail | Swoosh >

Tweet | Tweet >

By default, when you get a text message, you get an alert sound that lets you know it's there (if your iPhone's Ring/Silent switch isn't set to Silent, of course). If you'd rather not get an alert sound each time a text message comes in, you can turn it off by tapping on the Settings app, then tapping on Sounds, then tapping on **Text Tone** and it displays the sounds you can choose as your alert (by default, it's set to Tri-tone). To turn off the alert sound, just tap on None at the top. Now tap the Home button to close Settings.

---

iTip: Your iPhone Will Alert You

When you receive a message, your iPhone will sound an alert (provided you have that prefer-ence set in your Sounds settings). However, you may be away from your iPhone or unable to hear it in a noisy environment, so it will sound up to two more times (about three minutes apart) to remind you that you have a message waiting.

Seeing How Many Characters You've Typed

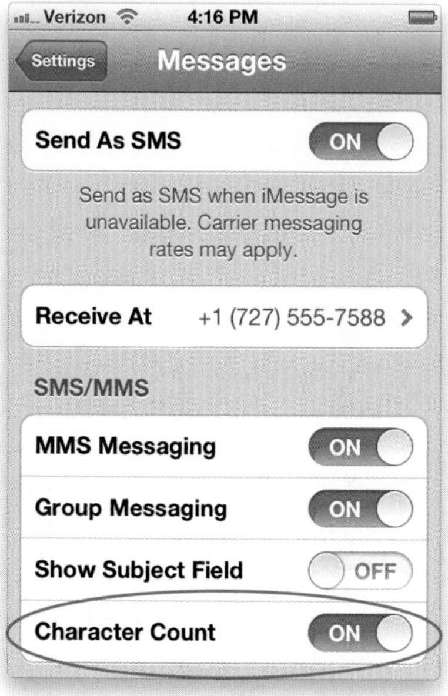

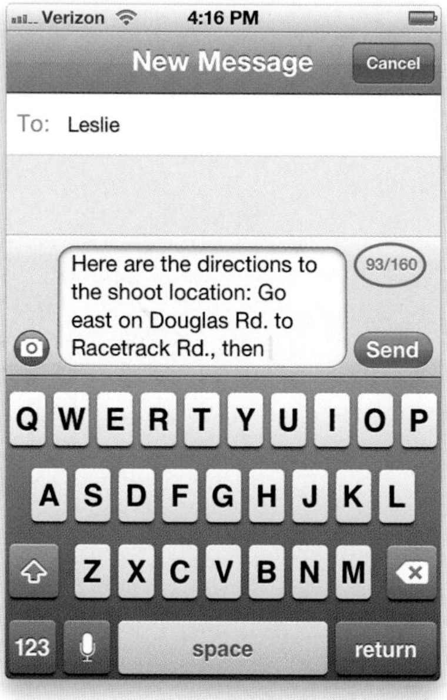

If you're typing a really long text message, your iPhone will tell you how many characters you've typed. You'll want to know this because there's a 160-character limit for a single SMS text. To turn on this feature, tap on the Settings app, then tap on Messages, and then tap the **Character Count ON/OFF button** to turn it on. Now, once you type more than 50 characters, a little character counter automatically appears next to the top-right corner of the message field, showing you how many characters you've typed.

Create Your Own Keyboard Shortcuts for Texting

If you're like me and wind up sending the same short text message fairly often (my favorite is "Running 10 minutes late"), you can add these as shortcuts, so you only have to type a few letters and it types in the full message for you. To create your own text shortcuts, tap on the Settings app, then tap on General, scroll down, and tap on Keyboard. At the bottom of the Keyboard settings you'll see a Shortcuts section (as seen above on the left). To create your own custom shortcut, tap the **Add New Shortcut button**, then type in the phrase (maybe something like "I'm driving---I'll text back in a few minutes"), then type the shortcut you want (maybe "drv"), then tap the blue Save button at the top right. Now when you type "drv," you'll see a little pop-up message displaying "I'm driving---I'll text back in a few minutes." If that's what you want to say, just tap the spacebar and it fills in the rest for you. Feel free to add as many shortcuts as you'd like (of course, now you have a new challenge—remembering all your shortcuts).

---

iTip: Have Your iPhone Flash Its Flash When You Get a Text Message

You can actually set your iPhone up so the LED flash for your camera will flash when you get a text message. Tap on the Settings app, then tap on General. Now, scroll down to Accessibility and turn on **LED Flash for Alerts**. That's it. Now when your iPhone's asleep and people text you, you'll visually see a flashing light. What happens if you're in a nightclub and someone texts you? Sadly, you'll never know.

Chapter Four
App Anthem
Using Apps & the App Store

 Believe it or not, I actually could have gone with the name "APP" or "A.P.P." for the name of this chapter, because apparently we have run out of decent names for bands and songs. APP is a band that has one song in the iTunes Store, "I'm on Fire," which is a cover of Bruce Springsteen's "I'm on Fire." I looked at the popularity ranking for "I'm on Fire" by APP, and it clearly was not, so then I looked at a song called "A.P.P." by a band called Papa Project, and it sounded like a harmless reggae-style background track, but I was afraid of what A.P.P. might actually stand for, so I went with a safer bet: "App Anthem," by Jimmy Towle/Doug Kaufman. "App Anthem" is actually a pretty decent sounding rap tune, and while it's certainly possible "App Anthem" may be littered with dirty words, I'll never know, because I couldn't make out a single word, but I don't feel bad because I'm pretty sure no one older than 14 has even a remote chance of deciphering them. In fact, I doubt that decryption experts at the CIA could figure out what's actually being said in your average rap song, which makes you wonder why other countries don't just have secret messages sent to their embedded field operatives via rap tunes. Think about it—the only way we'd be able to crack the code is if we were able to convince a 14-year-old to stop playing *Halo* long enough to write down what's being said. But, 14-year-olds don't write anymore, they text, and they use a shorthand for texting that only other 14-year-olds can possibly understand, and honestly, it would be easier for us to just to do the old "briefcase switcharoo" routine than it would be to find a 14-year-old that hasn't already been hired by the breakaway Republic of Irapistan. I miss the old days when we just used invisible ink.

Getting Apps from the iTunes App Store

You can get cool games, handy utilities, social networking apps—you name it—exclusively through the iTunes Store's App Store. A lot of them are free, and of the ones that do charge, the vast majority are only 99¢ to $1.99. The ones that cost more are usually under $10, but the most amazing thing is the quality of these apps—even the free ones. You can access the App Store from iTunes on your computer by just clicking on the App Store button at the top of the iTunes Store's homepage. This will take you to the App Store homepage, where you'll see featured apps, lists of the most popular apps, and of course you can search for apps using the Search Store field at the top right of the window, just like you do for songs or videos. Once you find an app that you want to download and use, you can click on it and then click the **Buy App button** (or the **Free App button**, if it's free). You'll see the price right next to the app and, again, many of them are free. Your apps will be downloaded to your computer and will appear in your Apps Library in your iTunes Source list. The next time you sync your iPhone to your computer, your new apps will be transferred to your iPhone (if you have this preference set).

> 📶 **iTip: Only Pay for Apps Once**
>
> *If you buy an app and then, for whatever reason, you delete it later, you can always redownload/re-install the apps you get from the App Store without paying for them again. They are tied to your Apple ID, and Apple knows which ones you get.*

Getting Apps from Your iPhone's App Store

You can also download apps wirelessly from your iPhone's App Store. Just tap on the App Store app and you'll be connected to the same App Store as if you were doing it via iTunes, however, this App Store is formatted specifically for your iPhone. You can browse the New or What's Hot Featured apps, or you can look through the Categories, or check out the Top 25 apps. If you know the name of the app you're looking for, you can tap Search and type the name of the app to search for it. You can also use the Genius feature here (more on using this with music in Chapter 11). Once you find an app you want to download to your iPhone, tap on it, then just tap the price (or Free) button, then tap the **Buy Now (or Install) button**, and you'll be asked to enter your Apple ID username and password. The app will be downloaded and installed directly on your iPhone. The next time you sync your iPhone with your computer, the app will be downloaded to your iTunes Apps Library (if you have that preference set).

---

iTip: Downloading Apps That Are Larger Than 20MB

Although you can download most apps using your iPhone's cellular data network, if a particular app you want to download is larger than 20MB in size, you'll have to jump on a Wi-Fi network to download this large a file.

Updating Your Apps in iTunes

To check to see if your apps have any available updates, just open iTunes on your computer and click on your Apps Library in the Source list on the left side of the window. Then, click the **Check for Updates link** in the bottom-right corner of the iTunes window, and if there are any updates available, you'll be taken to a screen that lists them, where you can then update your apps individually or all at once.

Updating Your Apps on Your iPhone

You can also get your iPhone app updates directly on your iPhone. Just tap on the App Store app and you'll see an Updates button in the lower-right corner with the number of apps on your iPhone that have had updates released. To see what features (or fixes) have been included in the update, tap on it. To download the update, just tap the **Update button** on the update's info screen. If you have multiple apps that have updates, you can download all of them at once by tapping Update All at the top right of the Updates screen.

Deleting Downloaded Apps from iTunes

If you decide that you no longer want a particular app, just click on its icon in your Apps Library in iTunes and hit the **Delete (PC: Backspace) key** on your keyboard. You'll then get a warning letting you know that if you delete the app from iTunes, it will also be deleted from your iPhone the next time you sync. Click the **Delete App** button and the next dialog will ask if you want to move the app to the Trash (PC: Recycle Bin). Click the Move to Trash (PC: Move to Recycle Bin) button and the next time you empty the Trash, the app will be deleted from your computer. Also, the next time you sync your iPhone, the app will be uninstalled from your iPhone (if you have that preference set).

Deleting Downloaded Apps from Your iPhone

Although you can't delete the apps put on your iPhone by Apple, you can easily delete apps that you've downloaded from the App Store. On the Home screen, tap-and-hold your finger on the app you want to remove. All of your icons will start to wiggle and you'll see an X appear in the upper-left corner of each app you downloaded from the App Store. Tap the **X** to remove the app from your iPhone. The next time you sync your iPhone, the app will also be removed from iTunes (if you have that preference set).

---

iTip: Viewing Your iTunes Store Account Info

*If you want to view or change your iTunes Store account info, you can do that right from your iPhone. Tap on the Settings app, then scroll down to Store. Now tap on Sign In, enter your Apple ID info, and you'll have access to your account info by tapping on your Apple ID and then tapping on **View Apple ID**. You can change your payment method, or even sign up to receive the store newsletter or special offers.*

Organizing Your Apps in iTunes

While it's great that I can rearrange my apps and make folders right on my iPhone (see the next page for more on making folders), when I have a lot of arranging to do, I prefer to do it on my computer in iTunes. iTunes lets you rearrange the order of the Home screens themselves just by clicking-and-dragging. So, if you have a lot of arranging to do, just connect your iPhone to your computer and select it in the iTunes Source list. Click on the **Apps tab**, and you can choose which apps to sync, as well as click-and-drag them into the order you want, or hover your cursor over an app and click on the X button at the top left to delete it. Once you're done, click the Apply button to sync your iPhone.

Moving Apps and Creating Folders on Your Home Screen

The iPhone has some very useful apps built in, but you may not need every app that's on your main Home screen. (For example, if you don't play games, you might not need the Game Center app there.) Although you can't delete these apps from the iPhone (the apps that come built in), you can move them off your main Home screen or put them in a folder. You can have up to 11 Home screens and 20 folders per screen containing 12 apps each. So, you can move less frequently used apps to another screen. To do this, tap-and-hold on any app for a few seconds until all the icons start to wiggle. Now, tap-and-drag the icon of the app you no longer want on your main Home screen to the right edge of the screen. This will switch the iPhone to the next Home screen. You can either release the icon there or drag it to the right edge again to advance to the third screen, and so on. Once you get to the screen that you want to put this app on, just release it there. When you've moved all the apps off the main Home screen that you no longer want to see there, then you can drag any app that you don't use regularly onto another app to create a folder. You can name the folder whatever you like. When you're finished rear-ranging all your apps, click the Home button to stop the icons from wiggling and lock in your changes.

Creating an App Folder in Your Dock

The Dock is at the bottom of each Home screen and the apps located in it are available no matter which Home screen you happen to be looking at. Apple placed the ones there that they thought you would want to have available at all times. For example, the Phone app is there and that makes sense. After all, the iPhone is a phone. But, I like to have access to more than just four apps from any Home screen, so I created a "Productivity" folder in the Dock containing 12 apps that I use regularly. Now I have a total of 15 Apps in my Dock that I can access no matter which Home screen I happen to be on.

---

iTip: Moving Between Home Screens

Since you can add Web clips and apps to the Home screen, the iPhone gives you up to 11 Home screens. Once you have two or more Home screens, you will see little dots above the Dock indicating how many Home screens you have, and which screen you're looking at (its dot appears white). You can either tap a dot to switch screens or you can flick the screens left or right like you do with pictures.

Where to Find the Very Coolest Apps

There are literally hundreds of thousands of apps in the iTunes App Store, and finding the coolest, most useful, best designed apps isn't easy. That's why every day I go to Terry's app website, because Terry has a gift for finding exactly those types of apps. Honestly, I don't know how he does it, but he always comes up with these amazing apps that everybody falls in love with (which is precisely why, when it comes to iPhone apps, Terry has built a huge cult following). Check it out at www.bestappsite.com.

Quickly Switching to Another App

iOS 5 supports both multitasking, as well as fast app switching. If an app supports either of these technologies you'll be able to toggle back and forth between multiple apps without having to close one and return to the Home screen first. Just double-click the Home button and the multitasking bar will appear at the bottom of the screen. Tap on the app you want to switch to and it will open. By default, you'll see the last four apps you used in the multitasking bar. However, you can scroll the bar to the right to see more.

Accessing Your Audio Controls While in Another App

Once you have music going in your Music app or any third-party audio app, like Pandora Radio, you can launch another app and the music will keep playing. However, if you want to control the music, you don't have to go back to the app to do this. You can access the controls widget by double-clicking the Home button and scrolling to the left in the multitasking bar at the bottom of the screen.

Chapter Five

Please
Mr. Postman

Getting (and Sending) Email

This is an incredibly important chapter, because email is incredibly important. If it weren't for the iPhone's ability to get email, I would have missed an amazing adventure. It all started with a desperate email from a Mr. Mabutuu, who (according to the email) had been a high-ranking government official in the small African nation of Nantango. I soon learned of the overthrow of his small, friendly government through a military coup that nearly cost him his life. He was able to flee to the safety of a small village protected by freedom fighters loyal to his ousted government, but before he fled the capital, he was able to move nearly $16 million of his government's surplus cash (in U.S. funds) to a small bank in a neighboring country. His main concern was that these funds not fall into the hands of the corrupt general who led the rebellion against him, and he asked if I would be so kind as to help him find a suitable U.S. bank where he could wire the $16 million. For my small role in providing my bank account number, username, password, and social security number, he would gladly share the $16 million with me rather than see it seized by the new hostile government (he proposed a 60/40 split, but I was able to negotiate it to 50/50). However, he was in a bind because before his bank would transfer the funds to my bank account, he would have to first pay $22,800 for the required doc stamps and tariffs to complete the wire transfer. Of course, I immediately wired the $22,800 to his overseas account, and since then, each day I patiently check my account for the transfer of the $16 million to hit (that's going to be a pretty exciting day for us both, eh?).

Setting Up Your Email

If your email is already set up on your computer, then you can choose in iTunes which email accounts you want to have working on your iPhone (click on your iPhone in the Devices list on the left of the window, then click on the Info tab in the iPhone's preferences and make your sync choices in the Mail Accounts section). To set up your email directly on your iPhone, tap on **Mail**, then on the Welcome to Mail screen, just tap on the type of email account you have if it's in the list. If your email account is on Apple's iCloud (or older MobileMe), Microsoft Exchange, Google (Gmail), Yahoo, AOL, or Hotmail, your iPhone will know most of the geeky settings, so all you'll need is your username, email address, and password (if you use iCloud or Microsoft Exchange, see pages 86 and 87). If your account isn't on one of these services, see the next page. By the way, if you have a Yahoo, Gmail, or Hotmail email account, you'll get a free "push" type email. This means that instead of having to check for new messages, the emails will come to your iPhone automatically. Some other types of accounts will need to be checked, which you can set your iPhone to do automatically at regular intervals. The iPhone software also has Microsoft Exchange Active Sync support, but you'll need to check with your company's IT department to get the settings first.

Setting Up an "Other" Email Account

If your email account isn't listed on the Welcome to Mail screen (see the previous page), scroll down and tap **Other** to set it up yourself. You'll need to know at least your username, email address, and password—the iPhone will know the geeky settings for most webmail accounts. If not, you'll need to know:

- your email server type: POP, IMAP, or Exchange
- incoming server address (a.k.a. POP server): mail.domain.com
- outgoing server address (a.k.a. SMTP server): smtp.domain.com

Also, most outgoing mail servers require some kind of password for sending mail when you're not on their network. You'll need to check with your ISP to find out what settings to use. Most ISPs display this info in the help section of their websites. When you set up your account, you probably received an email with all of this info.

---

iTip: Choose IMAP Over POP

If you have a choice between POP- or IMAP-based email, choose IMAP. The reason is that IMAP email resides on a server. When you read an email on your iPhone, it will be marked as read on the server so that when you go to your computer to check email, you won't have to read the ones you've already read. Same goes for trashing an email. Once trashed on the iPhone, it will be trashed on your computer, too.

Add an iCloud Email Account

....ll AT&T	8:43 PM	98%

Cancel | **iCloud** | **Next**

Apple ID   example@me.com

Password   Required

Forgot Apple ID or Password?

Learn more about iCloud

Get a Free Apple ID >

Apple has their own free service called iCloud, which offers direct push and syncing of your email similar to Microsoft Exchange. (You can also sync your contacts, Safari bookmarks, reminders, notes, music, photos, documents/data, and calendar to iCloud and have this information wirelessly sync to your iPhone. For more on iCloud, see Chapter 9.) iCloud includes an email account (.me) and when email is received in your iCloud account, if you want to, it can be pushed out to your iPhone instantly. iCloud is a cross-platform service for both Mac and Windows users. Once you have your iCloud account set up, you can set up your iPhone to receive your iCloud email by going to Mail and tapping on **iCloud** (if you haven't set up any other email accounts yet) or by going to Settings, then to Mail, Contacts, Calendars, then tapping on **Add Account**, and tapping on iCloud. Just enter your Apple ID and Password, and you're all set.

Add a Corporate Microsoft Exchange Email Account

```
.ıll... Verizon  3G      5:15 PM
┌─────────┐                   ┌──────┐
│ Cancel  │    Exchange       │ Next │
└─────────┘                   └──────┘

   Email        email@company.com

   Domain       Optional

   Username     Required

   Password     Required

   Description  My Exchange Account
```

You can have direct push of email, calendar appointments, and contacts wirelessly via Microsoft Exchange, without having to sync via the USB cable to your computer. You'll have to first check with your corporate IT department to get the correct settings for your account, and once you have this information, add the Microsoft Exchange account to your iPhone (if you haven't set up any other email accounts yet, go to Mail and tap **Microsoft Exchange**, or from Settings, tap on Mail, Contacts, Calendars, then tap on **Add Account**, tap on Microsoft Exchange on the Add Account screen, and enter your Exchange account information). You'll get the option of whether or not you want your contacts and calendar synced, too, and in iOS 4 and higher, there is support for multiple Exchange accounts. When email is received at your office, it is pushed out to your iPhone immediately. When someone proposes a meeting, you'll be able to respond and have the meeting added to your calendar instantly. Also, any changes to your contacts are automatically synced to the server. So you basically never have to sync this information via the USB cable. Don't throw the cable away just yet, though, you'll still need it to sync your iPhone for music, movies, etc., as well as for iPhone software updates (if you're not syncing all this wirelessly) and to charge it.

Checking Your Email

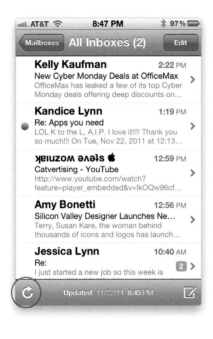

The iPhone is pretty smart in that there really isn't a check email button. It assumes that when you tap the Mail app on the Home screen, you probably want to check your email. Once you're looking at your Inbox, you can also have the iPhone check for new mail immediately by tapping the **curved arrow icon** in the lower-left corner of the screen. The iPhone can check for new email manually, on a schedule (such as every 30 minutes—just go to Settings, tap on Mail, Contacts, Calendars, then tap on **Fetch New Data**, and make your choice in the Fetch section), or if your email account supports it, via "push." For example, Microsoft Exchange and iCloud email is automatically pushed out to your iPhone as soon as it comes in.

---

iTip: Email Download Times and Your Battery

You can change your settings for Mail to automatically check for new messages every 15 minutes, every 30 minutes, or every hour. The more often the iPhone checks for email, the more it will use the battery. I chose every 30 minutes as a happy medium.

The Unified Inbox

In iOS 4 and higher, you can see email from multiple accounts all in one inbox with the All Inboxes combined inbox. This is one of my favorite features, since I have several email accounts on my iPhone. I can see, read, and respond to email from each of my accounts in one spot. You can get to the All Inboxes combined inbox by tapping on the **Mail app** or by tapping the **back button** from any email account you're currently in.

Reading Your Email

Once your email is set up and the messages start rolling in, tap on the Inbox you want to check. Unread messages will have a blue dot to the left of them and the iPhone displays the first two lines of each message. When you want to display the entire email, just tap on the one you want to read. You can scroll through the message by flicking your finger up or down on the screen. If the type is too small, you can use the pinch feature to zoom in and out: using two fingers on the display, such as your index finger and thumb, you spread them out to zoom in on the message, then pinch them in to zoom back out. You can also pan around the message by simply moving your finger around on the display in the direction you want the message to move. You can use the up and down arrows in the upper-right corner to move to the next message or previous message. In a text email, you can also double-tap on a word and, from the pop-up menu, choose to Copy of Define it.

---

iTip: Marking a Message as Unread

*You can mark a message that you are reading as unread by tapping the Details button in the upper-right corner of the message. You will then see a Mark button to the right of the subject header. Tap it, then tap the **Mark as Unread** button at the bottom and the message will stay marked as new.*

Threaded Email Discussions

You can view threaded email, and here's how it works: When you receive an email and then you or someone else responds back to it, and then another response from someone is sent, a thread is created. You'll actually see a little indicator with a message count on the right side of the email (when you're looking at it in your Inbox) and when you tap on the most recent message, you'll see all the messages relating to that email thread. This means no more having to scroll down through your Inbox to find the related messages that were sent earlier.

---

iTip: Is That Email Important?

*If someone sends an email message directly to you, chances are it's more important than an email that you were only copied on. The iPhone's Mail app lets you see if you are in the To field or in the CC field at a glance—a "To" or "Cc" will be at the beginning of each message that has you in one of these fields. If you don't see this, tap on the Settings app, then tap Mail, Contacts, Calendars, and turn **Show To/Cc Label** on.*

Viewing and Playing Email Attachments

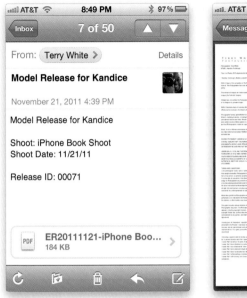

The iPhone supports viewing attachments such as JPGs, PDFs, Microsoft Office documents (Word, Excel, and PowerPoint), and iWork documents (Keynote, Numbers, and Pages). If you receive an image, such as a JPG, Mail shows the image right in the body of the message. If you receive one of the other file types, the attachment will generally be at the bottom of the email message. Simply tap the attachment to view it. The message will slide over to the left and show you the attachment in a separate screen. If you'd rather view the message in a different app that you have installed, you can tap the button with a box with an arrow coming out of it to transfer and view that attachment in a compatible app. If you prefer to see the attachment in a horizontal view, just turn your iPhone sideways. Once you're done viewing it, tap the Message button at the top of the screen to go back to the original email. If you have more than one attachment, you can view the next one once you return to the message. You can also play a compatible audio attachment (like an MOV or M4A file) by tapping on it in the email.

---

iTip: Printing an Email Attachment

*In iOS 5, you can print your email attachments through AirPrint. With the attachment open on your iPhone, simply tap the menu icon in the top-right corner, then tap the **Print button** in the menu that appears. For more on AirPrint, see page 104.*

Saving an Emailed Photo to Your iPhone

If you receive an email on your iPhone with a photo attached, you can add that photo to your iPhone's Camera Roll. Tap once directly on the image and a menu will pop up asking you to save or copy it, so just tap on **Save Image**, and it will be added directly to your Camera Roll. You can see the image you just saved in the Camera Roll by pressing the Home button, then tapping Photos, and then tapping **Camera Roll**. Once you see the image, tap on it to see it full screen and then you can set it as a wallpaper picture, email it to others, send it in a text message, assign it to a contact, tweet it, or print it by tapping on the image and then tapping on the little box with the arrow at the bottom left of the screen. (*Note:* For more on these options, see Chapter 13).

Dialing a Phone Number from an Email

If someone sends you an email that has a phone number in it, you can simply tap the phone number to dial it. A box will pop up with the number, and Call and Cancel buttons. Tap the **Call button**, and your iPhone will automatically switch over to the Phone app and place the call. Once you're finished with your call, you can tap the End button. This will take you back to your email message.

---

iTip: Saving or Sharing a Phone Number

If you want to add a phone number from an email to an existing contact, create a new contact with that phone number, or send a text message to it, just tap-and-hold on the phone number to bring up those options.

Going to a Website from an Email

The Web links in your email message, whether they are text links or links on images, are live. So tapping a link in an email will automatically fire up Safari (the Web browser app) and take you to the site that you tapped on in your email. Once you're done browsing the site, press the Home button twice to bring up the multitasking bar at the bottom of the screen, and then tap Mail to return to the message you were viewing. One of the features I really like about the Mail app is the ability to "hover my cursor" over a Web address in an email to see where that address really goes. Spammers and phishing scams often use hidden links under what looks like a legitimate address. Bring up the email with the questionable Web link in it, and simply tap-and-hold on the link for a few seconds. A menu will pop up showing the actual Web address the link will take you to, as well as Open, Copy, and Cancel buttons. This also works in Safari with links on webpages.

---

iTip: Bookmarking a Web Link

*Once you're in Safari and looking at the page you went to from the email message, you can bookmark it by tapping the menu button (it looks like a box with a curved arrow coming out of it) at the bottom of the screen, and tapping the **Add Bookmark button**. Once you add this Bookmark, it will be automatically synced back to your computer the next time you sync your iPhone (if you have this preference set).*

Replying to an Email

Tap the arrow pointing to the left in the toolbar at the bottom of the email (the second button from the right) and you will see a pop-up menu. You can choose Reply, Reply All (if the message was sent to more than one person), Forward, Print, or Cancel. When you tap Reply, you'll see a new message already addressed to the original sender and with the original subject. The cursor will already be in the body and all you have to do is start typing your reply. If the original message was sent to you and other people, you can tap the Reply All button to send your reply to the original sender and all the people that the message was sent or copied to. Once you've typed your reply, simply tap the Send button in the upper-right corner. If you tap the Cancel button, you can choose to save or delete the message.

---

iTip: Sending from a Different Account

*When composing a new message, you'll also see the Cc (carbon copy) and Bcc (blind car-bon copy) fields, and if you have multiple email addresses set up, you'll be able to choose which email address you want to send the reply from. Just tap in the Cc/Bcc, From field to activate the Cc and Bcc fields, and then tap in the **From field** to switch between email accounts for sending.*

Filing an Email in a Folder

If you have an IMAP-based email account set up, you can have access to additional folders you set up on your computer to help organize your messages, and you can move your email into any of these folders on your iPhone. Since IMAP account folders reside on a server, the next time you check email on your computer, the mail you moved on your iPhone will be in the folder you moved it to. To move a message to a folder, bring up the message from your Inbox and tap the **Move button** on the bottom toolbar—its icon looks like an arrow pointing down over a folder. You will see a list of folders you can move the message to. Tap the folder you want to move it to and your iPhone will move it. If you have a POP-based email account, you can still use this feature to move a message to the Drafts, Sent, or Trash folders. However, these folders only exist on your iPhone, so the message will not be moved to these folders on your computer.

---

iTip: Adding Punctuation Quickly

*Here's a tip we learned from our friend, author David Pogue: the secret to quickly adding any punctuation when using the keyboard is to tap-and-hold on the **number/punctuation button**, and in a moment, the number and punctuation characters will appear. Now just slide your finger over to the character you want and then remove your finger. It immediately returns you to the regular alphabetical keyboard. Thanks for sharing that one David—we use it every single day!*

Deleting, Moving, or Marking Emails

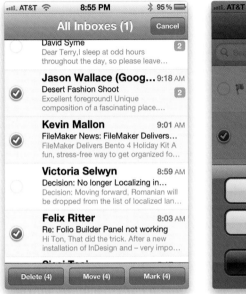
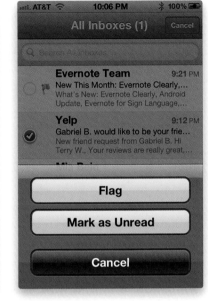

To delete messages from your Inbox, tap the Edit button at the top right and a circle will appear next to each message. You can tap the message you want to delete and the circle will turn red with a white checkmark. Once you've selected all the messages you want to delete, just tap the **Delete button** at the bottom left of the screen to delete them. You can move messages the same way: tap on the Edit button, then tap on the message(s) you want to move, and tap the **Move button** at the bottom of the screen. This will bring up a list of folders, and you can tap on the folder you want the message(s) moved into. In iOS 5, you can now also flag emails for later follow up, or mark them as read/unread in the same way. From any of your inboxes, just tap the Edit button, select the message(s) that you want to flag or mark, and tap the **Mark button** at the bottom right of the screen. In the menu that appears, just tap Flag or Mark as Read/Unread. Tapping Flag puts a visible flag icon to the left of the message(s). You can remove the flag the same way (the Flag button turns into Unflag).

---

iTip: Deleting a Single Message Quickly

*While you're reading a message, you can tap the **Trash icon** on the bottom toolbar to move the message to the Trash. If you get a message that you know you want to delete without even reading it, you can do it right from the Inbox by flicking your finger across the message. A **Delete button** will appear—tap it, and the message is gone.*

Searching and Handling the Results

Scroll up to the top of your Inbox, and you'll see a search bar. Tap in it, key in what you want to search for, and (new in iOS 5) tap the From, To, or Subject buttons to search in those fields, or tap All to search the entire body of your emails for any keywords or phrases that you want. To get rid of the keyboard, tap the Search button at the bottom right of it. Once your search results appear without the keyboard, you can tap the Edit button in the lower right of the screen, then select each message that you want to move (file away), delete, or mark by tapping on the circle in front of each one. Now, just tap either the **Delete**, **Move**, or **Mark button** to delete the messages, move them to a specific folder, or flag or mark them.

Forwarding an Email

To forward a message that you're viewing, tap the left-pointing arrow at the bottom of the screen. You will get a pop-up menu where you can choose Reply, Reply All (if the message was sent to multiple people), Forward, Print, or Cancel. Tap **Forward**, and the message appears ready for you to type in the name of the contact, or the email address, that you want to forward it to. If you start typing a name that is already one of your saved contacts, you will see a list of contacts to choose from. The more letters you type, the more it will narrow down the list. If you just want to choose a contact directly, you can tap the + (plus sign) button at the right side of the To field to choose one of your contacts. After putting in your first contact, if you want to forward this message to additional contacts, just start typing in a new name (or email address) and the list will pop up again for you to choose the contact that you want to forward this message to. You can also carbon copy (CC) or blind carbon copy (BCC) additional contacts.

Writing a New Email

To create a new email message, tap on Mail, then tap the **Compose button** at the bottom right of the screen. A blank email will appear with the cursor in the To field. You can then either type in the name of the contact or the email address that you want to send it to. If you start typing a name that is already one of your saved contacts, you'll see a list of contacts to choose from. The more letters you type, the more it will narrow down the list. If you just want to choose a contact directly, you can tap the + (plus sign) button at the right side of the To field to choose one of your contacts. If you want to send this message to additional contacts, just start typing in a new name. You can also carbon copy (CC) or blind carbon copy (BCC) additional contacts. Next, you'll want to type a subject in the Subject field, and then your message in the body field below. Your email can be as long as you like. Once you have your message addressed and composed, you can tap the Send button to send it. If you tap the Cancel button, you'll be given the opportunity to save it as a draft and continue it later.

iTip: The Secret .com Button in Mail

*Did you ever notice that there's a .com button on the Safari app's keyboard, but not in the Mail app? Well, there is one, it's just not obvious. If you want to end an email address with .com, .org, etc., just tap-and-hold on the **period key** until the choices pop up. Then slide your finger over and choose a domain ending. You can actually use this feature with any keyboard with a period key.*

Editing Your Email

In iOS 5, in the same pop-up menu with Cut/Copy/Paste, you can add a little formatting to your email, get word suggestions, get a word definition, or increase/decrease the text indent. For formatting, you can add bold, italics, or underlining to a word or phrase, as well as increase or decrease the indent (Quote Level) of a block of text (when typing a reply). Just tap on Mail, and then tap the Compose button or reply to an existing message. Start typing your email as usual, and when you want to add some formatting, just double-tap the word you want to format. If it's more than one word, you can use the blue handles to extend your selection. At the right end of this pop-up menu, you can tap Suggest… to get a word suggestion. There's a triangle button to the right of this. Tap it to show the rest of the choices: BIU, Define, and Quote Level. Tap on BIU, and you'll get a menu with Bold, Italics, and Underline; tap on Define to get a dictionary definition; or tap on Quote Level to choose Increase or Decrease.

---

iTip: Quote Only Part of an Email in a Reply

If you only want to quote part of the original email in your reply, select the portion you want to quote by double-tapping near the part of the email you want to include in your reply and dragging the handles around it. Then, tap the arrow pointing to the left at the bottom of the screen, and then tap the Reply button.

Emailing a Photo

You can email either the photos you take with your iPhone's camera or ones that are already in your photo Albums. To email a photo, tap Photos. If you want to send a photo that you took with your iPhone's camera, then it will be in the Camera Roll folder. If you want to send a photo that you synced from your computer, it will either be in the Photo Library or one of the albums that you brought over. Find the photo you want to send and tap on it. In the lower-left corner will be an arrow coming out of a box. Tap that button and you'll have the choice to Email Photo, send it in a Message, Assign to Contact, Use as Wallpaper, Tweet, or Print. Tap the **Email Photo button**. This will put your photo into the body of a new message. You can then address the message to the contact(s) that you want to send the photo to, give it a subject, and type some text in the body area above the image. When your message is ready, just tap the Send button to send it off.

---

iTip: Emailing Multiple Photos

*You can also email multiple photos by going to Photos and selecting the Camera Roll or a particular album. Once the pictures are being displayed, you can then tap the arrow-in-a-box button in the top-right corner. Next, tap the photos you want to send to select them (you can select up to five), tap the Share button, and then tap the **Email button**.*

Printing an Email

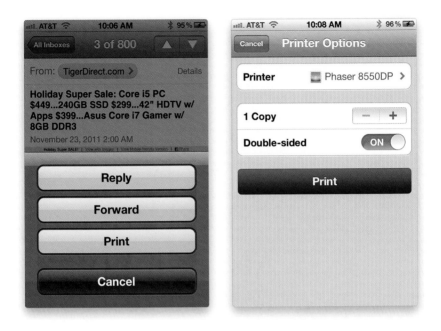

You can print your email to a wireless AirPrint-compatible printer directly from your iPhone (it must be connected to the same Wi-Fi network as your iPhone). Just bring up the email you want to print and tap the arrow pointing to the left in the toolbar at the bottom. This brings up a menu with Reply, Forward, and Print buttons. Once you tap **Print**, you'll be able to select your AirPrint-compatible wireless printer, choose how many copies to print, and print away.

---

iTip: When Your Printer Isn't AirPrint Compatible

Sadly, most printers are not AirPrint compatible. However, all is not lost. If you're on a Mac, you can use Printopia to turn your existing printer into an AirPrint-compatible printer. Check it out at: www.ecamm.com/mac/printopia/. If you're on a Windows PC, try AirPrint Activator at: http://twhite.me/tYinC5.

Sharing a Contact

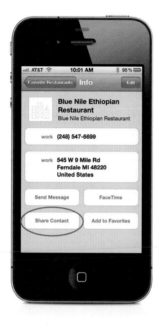

Tap on the Utilities folder, then tap Contacts, and find the contact that you want to share. At the bottom of their information, tap the button that says **Share Contact**, then choose to share it in an Email or a Message. Once you make your choice, the iPhone will create a vCard (an electronic business card) and attach it to a new message. You can then address the message to the person you want to send the contact to, and once they receive it, they can then import it into their contact manager or iPhone. If you receive a vCard from someone else, you can add that contact to your contacts list, as well.

---

iTip: Seeing Who an Email Is Addressed To

*If you are in an email, and tap on **Details** in the header, you can see the names or email addresses of the people the original message went to. If you tap one of the addresses (including the sender), and they are not already one of your contacts, you will be able to create a new email to that person, as well as add them to your contacts.*

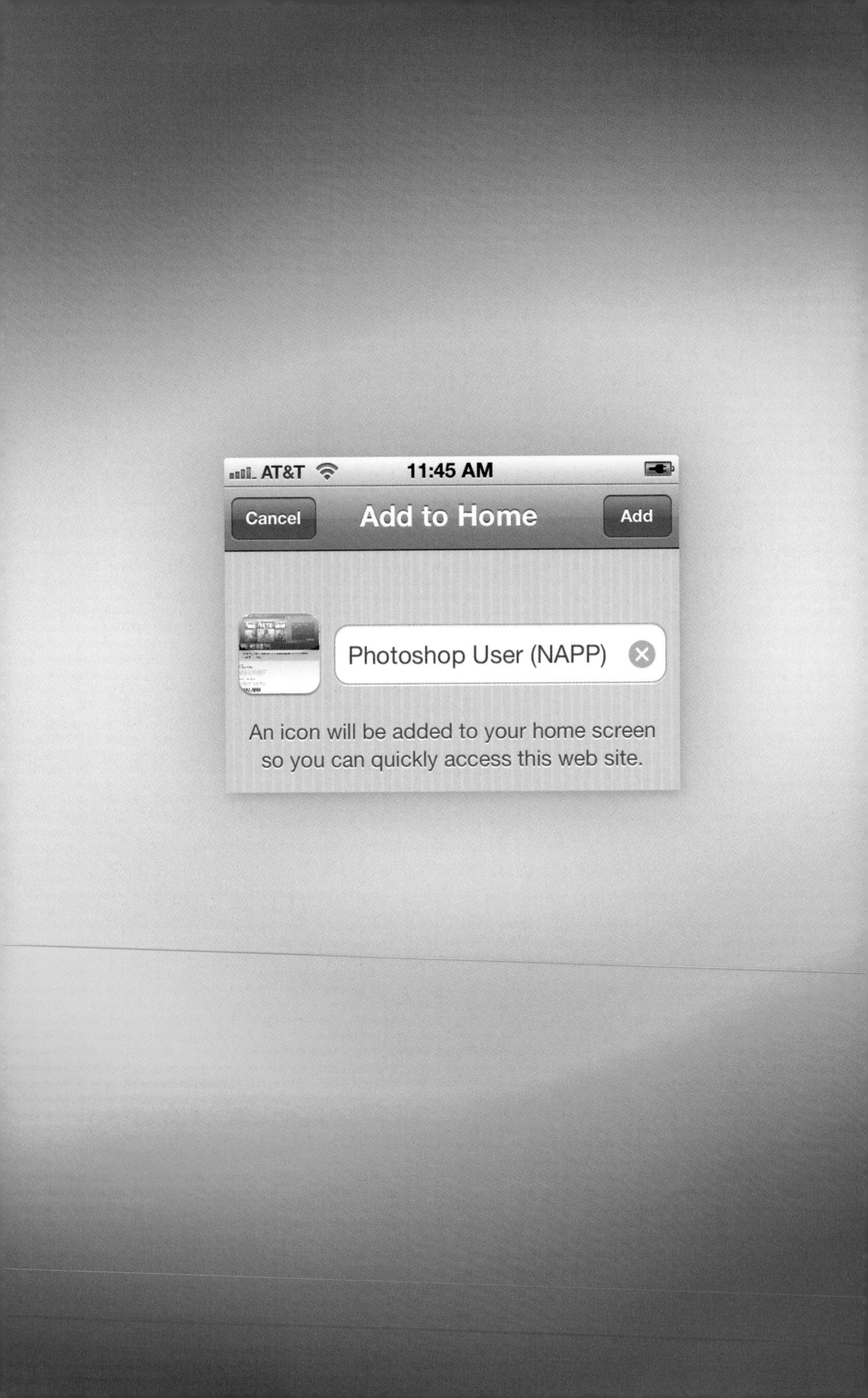
AT&T
11:45 AM
Cancel
Add to Home
Add
Photoshop User (NAPP)
An icon will be added to your home screen so you can quickly access this web site.

Chapter Six
Surfin' Safari

Using Safari, Your iPhone's Web Browser

Now you gotta admit—the Beach Boys' classic hit "Surfin' Safari" is just about as perfect a title for a chapter on using the Safari Web browser as you can get. But as you know, that's where the cohesiveness ends on this page, because the rest of this paragraph really has nothing to do with browsing the Web, or safaris, or even the iPhone for that matter. That's right, this is my "special time" where you and I get to bond on a level that I normally reserve only for close personal friends and men's room attendants. You see, when someone has read as much of this book as you have, a very magical thing happens. It's a magical moment of extreme clarity we both share simultaneously (but not at the same time), and although we experience this together, we do it totally separately, but still as one (which isn't easy to do). For example, it's that moment when you realize that you've already invested so much time in this book that you really can't stop now and you're "in it for the long haul." For me, it's the moment when I realize that you've had the book so long now you can't really return it for a refund. You see, it really is magical. So, put down the book, and take just a moment to close your eyes, breathe deeply, and just let your mind drift off to a place where it doesn't matter that the chapter introduction doesn't actually relate to the content in the coming chapter. That type of thing no longer matters to you because in your mind you're finally free—free to finally reach out and touch that existential neo-ocular nirvana that can only happen in Seattle. I have no idea how to end this gracefully. Hey! Quick—look over there!

Visiting Webpages on Your iPhone

Safari is the iPhone's Web browser (its app icon looks like a compass—it's shown circled here). The first time you launch Safari, it will launch to a blank screen with an Address Bar at the top. Tap in the Address Bar to bring up the keyboard and type in the Web address that you want to go to. There is a .com button on the keyboard to type in .com for you at the end of a Web address (it's a handy time saver). Once you have the address typed in, just tap the blue **Go** button. If you want to type in a different Web address, you can clear the address already in the Address Bar by tapping the little X to the right of it. Safari also will launch automatically when you tap on a Web address in one of the other apps.

---

iTip: Finding a Wireless Network

Your Web and email connections will be faster if you can jump on a wireless network, but finding a free wireless connection when you're on the road isn't easy, unless you know this trick: Go to the Maps app and type in "wifi." Then, if you don't have your Location Services turned on, a comma, and the city and state you're in (i.e., wifi, Kennebunkport, ME), and it will pinpoint the location of nearby places with free Wi-Fi. There's also a website called JiWire Wi-Fi Finder, which looks and acts like an iPhone app, and can search for not only local free spots, but any open Wi-Fi networks. Check it out at http://iphone.jiwire.com, where you'll also find a link to download the actual iPhone app for free.

Getting Around a Webpage

Once you get to a webpage, here are some tips for getting around: First, to scroll down the page you actually use your finger to flick the page up. In most cases, the page will be too small to read, but you can quickly zoom in on a page by double-tapping on it. This will zoom the display nice and large. To move the page around, just use your finger to drag the page in the direction that you want to go. To zoom out, double-tap the page again. You can also use two fingers in a spreading out motion as if you're expanding the size of the page to zoom in. To zoom out, use your two fingers to pinch the page as if you're making it smaller, because you are.

---

iTip: Jumping to the Top of the Page

If you've scrolled down a long page, tapping on the time at the top of the screen will take you back up to the top of the webpage.

Saving Webpages to Read Later

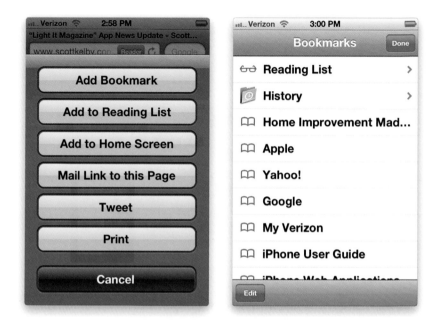

If you see a webpage you'd like to read, but you just don't have the time right this minute, then just tap the center button at the bottom of the Safari browser (the square button with the arrow), then tap **Add to Reading List** on the menu that pops up, and it saves that page for later. To see the pages you've saved to your Reading List, just tap on the Bookmarks button (at the bottom of your browser—its icon looks like an open book), and at the top of the list of Bookmarks, you'll see Reading List (with a pair of glasses to the left of it). Tap on that to see the list. *Note:* It just saves the link to these pages. You can't read them offline—you'll need to have Internet access to get to them.

---

iTip: Open Links in the Background

*When you tap-and-hold on a link in the Safari browser, a pop-up menu lets you open that link on a new page, but if you'd prefer to stay on the same page, and let that new page load in the background (so you can go to it when you're ready, and its fully downloaded), then just go to the Settings app, scroll down, and tap on Safari. Tap on Open Links, and choose **In Background**. That's all there is to it, and now you'll get the choice to Open in Background.*

Getting a New Page and Closing a Page

To get a new page, tap the little Pages icon in the lower-right corner of the Safari screen. This will shrink your current page down and a **New Page button** will appear in the lower-left corner. Tap that button to create a new blank page. Now you can either type in a new Web address, do a search, or use your Bookmarks to go to the page you want to go to. When you're finished viewing a page, there is no reason to have it out there hanging around, so to close a page that you no longer need open, tap the Pages icon, find the page you wish to close, and tap the little red X in the upper-left corner of the page. The page will close and you'll be switched to a page that is still open.

---

iTip: Handy One-Button Shortcuts

The next time you're typing a Web address into the Address Bar using the keyboard, take a quick glance at the Spacebar. That's right—there is no Spacebar (because Web addresses don't use spaces), but in its place is a one-button shortcut for .com, plus a Forward Slash key, and a Period key (all handy stuff you need when entering Web addresses).

Moving Between Pages

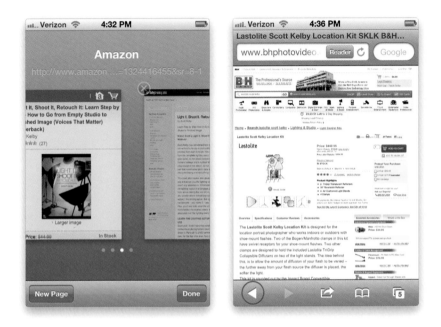

Once you have two or more pages open in Safari, you can move back and forth between them. To go to another open page, tap the **Pages icon** in the lower-right corner of the screen. Then, by flicking your finger across the page toward the left or the right, you can move between your open pages. Once you get to the page you want to view, just tap it to bring it back up to full screen. This is really handy when you're trying to compare things such as prices or schedules between two different sites at once. Also, Safari has a Back button just like any other Web browser—but here it's at the bottom of the screen (it's shown circled on the right here). There's also a Forward button if you want to return to the page you were just on.

iTip: See Where That Link Will Take You

If you press-and-hold your finger down on a text link or graphic link on a webpage, a pop-up menu will appear showing the Web address that the link will take you to, and giving you the option to Open, Open in New Page, Add to Reading List, or Copy.

Using Your Bookmarks

Your iPhone automatically syncs your Bookmarks from Safari on your Mac or PC, or your Favorites in Internet Explorer on your PC (if you have this preference set). To use one of these Bookmarks, tap the little **Bookmarks icon** at the bottom of the Safari screen (it looks like a little open book). All of your Bookmarks will be listed just as they appear on your computer. They'll be in the same folders and in the same order. Just go to the Bookmark you want to use and tap it to go to that site.

iTip: Refreshing a Webpage

Safari keeps the page you're currently viewing in place when you switch between apps. However, if you find that you want to know the latest bid on that eBay item you're watching, you may need to refresh the page. You can refresh just about any page in Safari by tapping the circular arrow button at the right of the Address Bar.

Adding a Bookmark

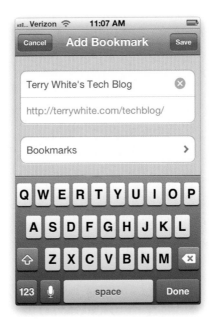

If you have a page open in Safari you'd like to bookmark, tap the center button (it looks like a box with an arrow) at the bottom of the Safari screen and, from the options that appear, tap the **Add Bookmark button**. This will ask you to name the Bookmark (you can simply leave it as the name of the page as it appears, or you can rename or shorten the name to your liking). You can also decide where it saves the Bookmark in your Bookmarks folders by tapping on the Bookmarks button below the Web address. Once you're happy with the name and location of the Bookmark, tap the Save button to save it.

iTip: You Don't Have to Type the Full Address

It's usually not necessary to type the full address, such as http://www.creativesuitepodcast .com. Usually just typing the domain name and domain extension will work, such as creativesuitepodcast.com.

Editing or Deleting a Bookmark

If you want to update or delete a Bookmark, launch Safari and tap the Bookmarks button at the bottom of the screen. This will bring up your Bookmarks list, where you'll be able to find the Bookmark that you want to edit or delete. Next, tap the **Edit button** in the lower-left corner of the Bookmarks screen (or the folder's screen, if it's in one). Then tap the Bookmark you wish to edit. You'll be able to edit the name and the Web address, as well as its location, then tap the Done button. When you tapped the Edit button, a – (minus sign) in a red circle appeared to the left of each Bookmark. To delete a Bookmark, tap the red circle next to it, and the Delete button will appear. Tap the **Delete button** and that Bookmark will be deleted forever. Once you've made your changes and deletions, tap the Done button, then tap the Bookmarks (or Bookmarks folder) button in the upper-left corner of the screen to return to the Bookmarks list.

---

iTip: Bookmark Changes Will Sync with Your iPhone

One great thing is that if you update or delete a Bookmark on your computer, it will be updated or deleted in your iPhone the next time you sync (if you have this preference set) or over the air if you use iCloud.

Adding or Removing a Direct Web Link Icon

If there are websites you go to a lot, you can add a Web link icon (Apple calls these Web clips) directly to your Home screen, and you can even have it scroll to the area of the page that you always check out. Just go to Safari, then go to the website you want to add (zoom in on it if you like), and tap the center button (it looks like a box with an arrow) at the bottom of the screen. From the options that pop up, tap on **Add to Home Screen**, and you'll see the screen shown on the left above, where you name your new icon. So, just name it and tap the Add button at the top right, and your new icon will be added to your Home screen. If the website is iPhone-aware, your icon will be the site's logo. If not, it'll be a mini version of the page. To remove a Web clip, tap-and-hold for a few seconds on it, until all the icons start to wiggle. You'll see a little X in the upper-left corner of each Web clip (and app that can be removed). Simply tap the little X and then tap **Delete**. The Web clip will disappear, and your remaining icons will reshuffle. Tap the Home button to stop the icons from wiggling and lock them in place.

---

iTip: Zooming In for Easier Scrolling

If you're on a webpage that is long and requires scrolling, you can of course flick your finger to scroll the page, or you can double-tap to zoom in on the page and then double-tap in the lower half of the page to scroll down a screen at a time (just be sure to tap in a blank area of the page).

Using Google Search

The iPhone is set to Google's search engine by default, and to use it, launch Safari, then tap on the search field (to the right of the Address Bar) to bring up the keyboard. Now, begin typing in your search terms and as you type, Google will offer suggestions. If you see what you want, just tap on it. If not, just tap the **Search button** in the bottom right when you finish typing. Once your search results come up, you can then tap on any of the links to go to the page that you want to visit. You can also make Yahoo or Bing the default search engine by changing your preference in the Safari settings (tap on the Settings app, then tap Safari, and choose Yahoo or Bing as your **Search Engine**).

---

iTip: Emailing a Website Link

*If you want to send a website link to someone, just tap on the center button (it looks like a box with an arrow) at the bottom of the Safari screen, then tap **Mail Link to this Page**, and it will create a new email with the Web address that was in the Address Bar in the body of the email message.*

Mobile Versions of Your Favorite Sites

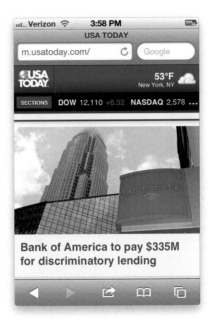

Many major websites have a "mobile" version or even a version specifically formatted for the iPhone. This makes getting to the information you want *much* faster! For example, I've optimized my blogs for mobile devices. If you visit www.terrywhite.com or www.bestappsite.com from your iPhone, you'll get the more friendly mobile versions of the websites. Check your favorite site to see if they have a mobile version. Oftentimes, it's as simple as typing "mobile" or "m" in front of the domain name, such as mobile.fandango.com or m.usatoday.com. You may be surprised to see that they even have one that's formatted just for your iPhone.

---

iTip: .org and Other Domains Are One Tap Away

Not every site ends in .com, but luckily, you can use the .com button to access the rest of the most commonly used domains on the Internet. If you want to use a different domain ending (such as .org), tap-and-hold on the .com button on the Safari keyboard and, once the choices pop up, slide your finger over them and choose the one you want.

Reading Webpages Made *Much* Easier

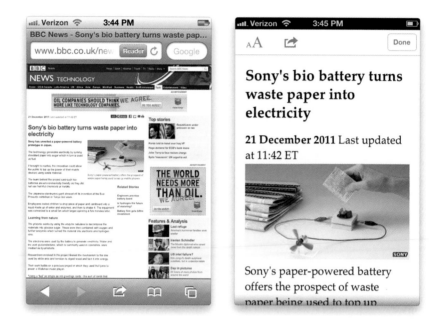

Reading articles on webpages packed with photos, and graphics, and banners, and... well, you get the idea, can be a bit challenging, which is exactly why you'll want to get to know Safari's built-in Reader. When you're starting to read an article, look to the right side of the Address Bar and you'll see a **Reader button**. Tap on it, and it hides all the extra stuff and gives you just the nice, clean, easy-to-read view you see above right. Plus, if you want the type larger, just tap on the "A" button at the top left of the screen to increase the font size (making it even easier to read).

---

iTip: Share Cool Sites You Find in Safari Directly to Twitter

*Twitter is pretty well integrated into Safari (see Chapter 14 for more info), and if you come across a site or a page you want to share with your followers on Twitter, all you have to do is click the center button (the box with the arrow in it) at the bottom of the screen, and in the pop-up menu that appears, tap the **Tweet button**. A little Twitter message window will appear right over Safari, where you can type in your message (the page's URL will automatically be included). It even counts the number of characters, so you don't go over the limit. When you're done, tap the Send button and your tweet, complete with the page's URL, is posted.*

Dialing a Phone Number on a Webpage

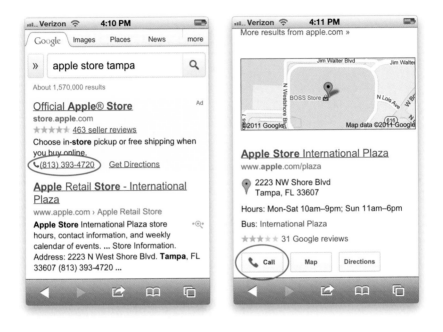

If you're looking at a webpage that has a phone number on it, chances are your iPhone will recognize it as a phone number and it will be highlighted or show up as a Call button. You can tap the **phone number** or **Call button** and your iPhone will ask you whether or not you want to dial it. If you tap Call, it calls that number. Once you tap End Call, you'll be returned to the webpage you were looking at last.

📶 **iTip: Open a Link in Safari to a New Page**

If you tap a link on a webpage, Safari will open that link in the same page you were just viewing. But, if you tap-and-hold on a link, you'll get the option to open that link in a new page. This way you can go back and forth between the two webpages.

Viewing RSS Feeds

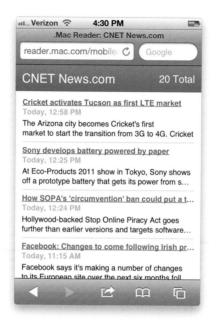

On your computer, use Safari (available for both Mac and PC) and go to some of your favorite websites. You will see an RSS button at the right side of the Address Bar if the site has a feed. Click the RSS button to take you to the feed page for that particular site. This is the page you'll want to bookmark. I place all my RSS feeds in a folder called (wait for it) "RSS" on my Bookmarks Bar. When you're done setting up your RSS folder, sync your computer and your iPhone to update your Bookmarks. Now when you're on your iPhone, you can tap any feed in that folder to see all the current headlines for that website.

iTip: Do Your Browsing in Private

*If you want to use Safari, but for security or privacy reasons you don't want there to be a history of what you view, just turn on Private Browsing (go to the Settings app, tap on Safari, then tap on the **Private Browsing Off button** to turn it on).*

Filling in an Online Form

When you get to a form on a webpage, you can tap on the first field on that page to zoom in on the field and bring up the keyboard. Type out your response for the first field, and then if the second field is still in view, just tap it and keep typing. If the next field is not in view, tap Done on the keyboard to zoom the page back out again, then you can tap in the field you want to go to next and the keyboard will reappear. You can also use the Previous and Next buttons to move from field to field. If you tap on a pop-up menu on a page, Safari does something very cool: it magnifies the list of choices and puts them in a flick wheel that you can spin with your finger to get to the right option. Once you've got your form all filled out, you can get rid of the keyboard or flick wheel by tapping Done and then tap the submit button for your form to submit your data.

---

iTip: Use the AutoFill Feature

*When you fill out a form that you'll be filling out on a regular basis, you can use the AutoFill feature to fill out the form with information from the last time you filled it out. To turn on this feature, tap on the Settings app, then tap on Safari, and then tap on **AutoFill**.*

Save or Copy an Image from a Webpage

If you find an image on a webpage that you want to keep, you can save the image directly from the webpage to your iPhone's Camera Roll (where you can then email it, send it in a text message, assign it to a contact, use it as your wallpaper, tweet it, or print it), or you can copy it to paste in another app. In the Safari app, just go to the webpage that has the picture on it that you want to save or copy, tap-and-hold on the picture, and a menu will pop up with the options to save or copy the image. Once you make your choice, the menu will go away and the image will be saved in your Camera Roll or copied to your clipboard. Access the image in your Camera Roll by tapping on the **Photos app**, or go to another app (like Mail), double-tap, and then tap the **Paste button** to paste it.

Chapter Seven
Tool Time
iPhone's Tools for Organizing Your Life

 Are we now to the point that our lives have become so complex, so chaotic, and so congealed (congealed?) that the only way to keep track of it all is to buy a hand-held device which becomes the center around which our lives revolve as it shouts out alarms, and commands us to be in certain places at certain times? All this while we're trying to monitor the markets, and stay in contact with people on different continents, in different time zones, and the only way we feel we can find the location of the nearest coffee shop is to send a request to a satellite in geosynchronous orbit above the earth requesting that it not only point out the location of said coffee shop, but that it ping a different satellite to provide a detailed photographic image of its roof? Is this what we've come to? Yes, yes it is, but I'm totally okay with it. Why? Because I bought stock in numerous GPS satellite companies, Google, and Starbucks. Okay, I really didn't buy stock in those companies but I could have, and I could have done it right from my iPhone. Well, at least until my wife found out, because at that moment you would've heard that cast-iron sound of a frying pan connecting with a husband's head (the one you hear in cartoons), but it would've been so loud that they would've heard it aboard the International Space Station (which is in geosynchronous orbit high above the earth, by the way), and when the astronauts heard it, they'd look at each other, nod, and say, "I bet some guy's wife just found out he bought a whole bunch of stock using his iPhone." You know, it really is a small world after all.

Using the Notification Center

iOS 5 includes a great new, somewhat hidden, Notification Center. It's available no matter which Home screen you're on or which app you're in. In the past, if an app gave you a Push notification, a little banner would appear onscreen that you had to acknowledge. Sometimes these notifications would interrupt the app you were in and, worse, if you got a lot of them while you were away from your iPhone, you'd have to go through and acknowledge each one before being able to do anything else. That has all changed. If you get a notification while you're doing something on your iPhone, it will appear briefly at the top of the screen and then go away. If your iPhone is asleep, you'll get an alert on the lock screen. Swipe the icon in the alert to the right to be taken to that app. If you ever want to see your notifications, just swipe down from the top of your screen to display your current and past notifications. Any apps that are configured to use the Notification Center will list their notifications there. You can clear all the notifications for a particular app by tapping the X, then tapping the Clear button for that category.

---

iTip: Change What You See in the Notification Center

You can choose which apps display notifications in the Notification Center, as well as reorder them in the list, by going to the Settings app and choosing Notifications. Tap the Edit button to be able to drag them in order. To turn off the notification or change the style of notification for an app, just tap on it in the list.

Using Reminders

iOS 5 includes a dedicated Reminders app, like a built-in to-do list. In the Reminders app, you can create new reminders by tapping the + (plus sign) button in the top-right corner. Then, just type your reminder and tap Done. Simple reminders will appear in your list with an empty checkbox by them. Once you complete the task, just tap the box to add a checkmark to it. If you want reminders that actually remind you to do something, tap on the reminder in the list, then tap on Remind Me. You can choose a particular day, or even set up a location reminder (location reminders don't work with Microsoft Exchange accounts, and if you have reminders turned on in your Mail settings, you'll need to turn them off). Location reminders are cool because they pop up to remind you when you arrive or leave a location of your choosing. You can also set priorities for your reminders to order them in the list, create multiple lists, and if you have a free iCloud account, your reminders will sync there.

---

iTip: Create New Reminders Lists

*To create a new Reminders list (i.e. Home, Work, Grocery, etc.), on the Reminders screen, tap the button in the top left that looks like three horizontal lines, then tap the Edit button in the top right. Tap **Create New List** and type in a list name. You can change lists by swiping side-to-side.*

Using Newsstand

Although most electronic magazine reading is probably done on the iPad, that doesn't mean that users won't want to read them on the iPhone, too. Luckily, in iOS 5, you can consolidate all your iPhone-compatible publications in one spot called Newsstand. Many of these publications are free, and most that cost include a free first issue, so that you can check it out. The easiest way of finding iPhone-Newsstand-compatible publications is to head to the Newsstand category of the App Store on your iPhone (or in iTunes). There, you will see all of the iPhone-Newsstand-compatible apps in one place. Once you download one of these, it will appear in your Newsstand. If the app supports subscriptions, new issues will appear in the same place, as they are available. One thing you'll note is that Newsstand acts like a folder for these apps. Therefore, Newsstand can't be put into a folder that you create, because technically it already is one.

---

iTip: Use Siri to Create Reminders

If you have an iPhone 4S, you can actually use Siri to create reminders for you. Just say something like, "Remind me to call my sister when I get home," and Siri will set up a location-based reminder for you automatically.

Using the Game Center

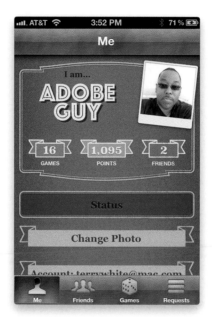

Gaming on the iPhone/iOS platform is big business. Games are often at the top of the App Store's most popular apps lists. Since games are so popular, often people want to not only play games, but they want to play games with or against their friends. This is where Game Center comes in. Game Center allows you to log in or create an ID and invite friends to be your online gaming buddies. From there, you can see all your Game Center–compatible games, share scores, challenge friends to play multiplayer games, and see your ranking against all that play a particular game. One of the games I play is Fruit Ninja, and it uses Game Center as its way of hosting a multiplayer game with another Fruit Ninja player.

Setting Up Clocks for Different Time Zones

Tap on the Clock app, then tap on **World Clock** at the bottom-left corner of the screen. By default, the World Clock screen shows the current times in Cupertino, California and New York. To delete a clock (we'll delete Cupertino's clock here), tap the Edit button in the upper-left corner, and a red circle with a – (minus sign) appears before each city. Tap the red circle for the one you want to delete and a Delete button appears on the right. Tap Delete and it's gone (the clock—not Cupertino itself). To add a new city, tap the + (plus sign) button in the top-right corner to bring up a city search field and keyboard. Type in the city you want to add (in our example here, I typed in Los Angeles. Actually, I just typed in "los" and Los Angeles, U.S.A., appeared in the list). When your city appears in the list, just tap on it and it's added as a clock. To add more cities, just tap the + button again.

---

iTip: Why the Default Time Is Cupertino

Why does one of the default clocks in the World Clock screen show Cupertino, California? It's because that's where Apple's headquarters (also known as "the mothership" to Macintosh fanatics) is located.

Using the Stopwatch

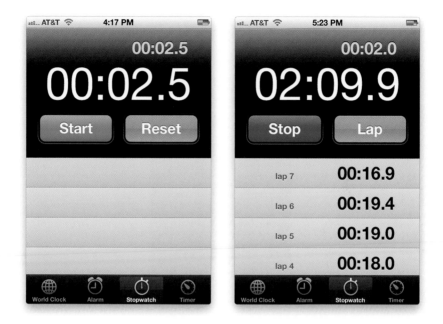

In the Clock app, tap on **Stopwatch** at the bottom of the screen to bring up the Stop-watch screen. There are only two buttons: Start and Reset. To start timing something, tap the green Start button. Once the stopwatch starts running, the green Start button is replaced by a red Stop button. To start over, tap Stop, then tap the Reset button. If you want to record lap times, just tap the Lap button (what used to be the Reset button before the stopwatch started running), and those times are listed in the fields below the two buttons. You can have lots of individual lap times (I stopped at 32 laps—man, was I tired), and you can scroll through the list of lap times just like you would scroll any list—by swiping your finger on the screen in the direction you want to scroll.

---

iTip: How to Tell It's Nighttime

When you're looking at the time in the World Clock screen, if the clock's face is white, that means it's daytime in that city. If the clock's face is black, it's night.

Setting Up a Countdown Clock

If you need to count down a particular length of time (let's say you're baking and you need to know when it's been 15 minutes), you can set a countdown timer to alert you after 15 minutes has passed. To do this, in the Clock app, tap on **Timer** at the bottom-right corner of the screen to bring up the Timer screen. You can scroll the Hours and Minutes wheels onscreen to set the amount of time you want to count down to. Just below the countdown wheels is a button called When Timer Ends, where you choose either the ringtone that your iPhone will play when the countdown clock hits zero, or you can choose to have the iPhone simply go to sleep (which is great if you want to play music for a specific amount of time before you fall asleep, and then have the iPhone put itself to sleep to save battery life). Once you've set your countdown time, and selected what happens when the timer hits zero, just tap the green Start button and the count-down begins.

---

iTip: Siri Can Count Down for You

Siri, on the iPhone 4S, knows about the built-in timer. Just ask Siri to "Set a timer for 35 minutes" (or whatever amount of time you want), and Siri will set and start the timer.

Using Your iPhone as an Alarm

In the Clock app, tap on **Alarm** at the bottom of the screen to bring up the Alarm screen. To add an alarm, tap on the + (plus sign) button up in the top-right corner of the screen. This brings up the Add Alarm screen, where you can choose whether, and how often, to repeat this alarm, what sound will play when the alarm goes off, whether to allow you to snooze the alarm, and the name of the custom alarm you just created (that way, you can save multiple custom alarms, which is handy if you have to wake up at different times on different days). When you've set up your alarm the way you want it, tap Save and your alarm appears in your Alarm list, and it's turned on. At the set time, your alarm sounds (and will keep sounding) until you tap on the Snooze button (if you turned that feature on), tap-and-slide the Slide to Stop Alarm button, or press the Sleep/Wake button at the top of your iPhone. If you tap Snooze, the alarm sound stops, but it will re-sound in 10 minutes. If you Slide to Stop Alarm or press the Sleep/Wake button, it turns the alarm off. Also, if you want to turn on an alarm you've already set, you can turn on/off alarms in the Alarm list.

---

iTip: Use Siri to Set an Alarm

If you have an iPhone 4S, you can actually ask Siri to set an alarm for you. Siri understands commands like, "Wake me at 7:30 a.m." Siri will set the alarm and confirm it with you.

Using the Calculator

When you tap on **Calculator** in the Utilities folder, it will bring up a basic calculator. This calculator does all the basic functions that you would expect, such as add, subtract, multiply, and divide, and it has a built-in memory function, too. If you want a more sophisticated scientific calculator (with sine, cosine, tangent, logarithm, etc.), just turn your iPhone sideways and you'll get the Scientific Calculator instead of the basic one. Pretty neat!

---

iTip: Clearing Calculator Mistakes

If you make a mistake while entering a series of numbers, you don't have to start over again. Just tap the C key once and that will perform a Clear Entry, and then you can simply re-enter the number. Also, to delete an individual number you typed by mistake, just swipe your finger over the display and the last number you entered will be deleted.

Finding Videos on YouTube

You can watch videos from the online video sharing site YouTube.com right from your iPhone. It doesn't actually download the videos from YouTube.com onto your iPhone—you search for videos you want to watch, and then you watch them on your iPhone just like you would watch YouTube.com videos on your computer (however, you can save videos as Favorites, so you can get right to them. See page 137). Start at the Home screen and tap on YouTube. Then tap on **Search** (at the bottom of the screen) to bring up a search field. Tap on the search field to bring up the keyboard, type in your search term(s), then tap the Search button to search YouTube's vast video library. The results appear in a list below the search field. To watch one of these videos, just tap on it, then turn your iPhone sideways for a larger view. To see more about a video in the list, tap the blue arrow button to the right of the video in the results list. You can also go directly to YouTube's Featured videos of the day and the Most Viewed videos by tapping the buttons at the bottom of the screen. If you tap the More button, you'll see a set of menus that let you jump to YouTube's Most Recent videos, or see their Top Rated videos, a History (list) of the YouTube videos you've already watched, the YouTube videos you've posted, the YouTube videos you subscribe to, and your YouTube Playlists.

Playing YouTube Videos on Your iPhone

When a video first starts playing, a set of controls appears onscreen for pausing the video, adjusting the volume, etc. There's even a button to email a YouTube video link to a friend or tweet it. To bring back those controls, just touch the screen. To return to the search results list, tap the blue Done button in the top-left corner, then on the More Info screen for the video, tap the button in the top left with the video's name. On the next screen, you will find related videos, or you can tap the Search button at the top left to get back to your Search screen.

Saving YouTube Videos as Favorites

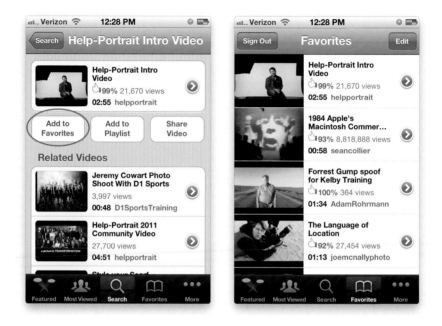

To add a video you like to your Favorites (so you can jump directly to it next time), you'll need a YouTube account. You'll have to create that account on your computer at www .youtube.com. Once you've got your username and password, you can then sign into your YouTube account on your iPhone. This way, when you save favorites either on your iPhone or on your computer, they'll be saved in both places. Once you find a video that you like, you can add it to your Favorites by tapping the **Favorites button** (it looks like a book) while the video is playing, or by tapping the **Add to Favorites button** beneath the YouTube video's info (tap the Done button after playing the video, then tap the button in the upper-left corner with the video's name on it to get to the info screen). Once you've added videos to your Favorites, you can tap the Favorites button at the bottom of the screen to view the list and play any of your favorite videos whenever you like.

Customizing the YouTube Buttons

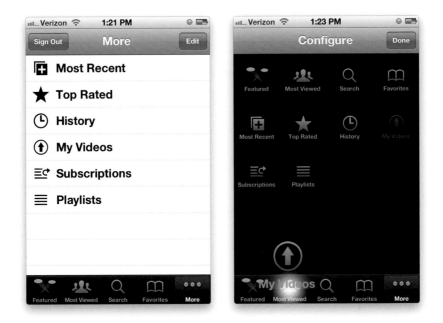

Although a default set of buttons appears in a bar at the bottom of the main YouTube screen, you can customize this bar to contain the YouTube buttons you use the most. To do this, tap on the YouTube app, then tap the **More button.** When the More screen appears (and you see the row of buttons across the bottom), tap the Edit button in the top-right corner of the screen to bring up the Configure screen. Now you just press-and-hold your finger on any button you'd like to appear on your bar, and simply drag it down to the bar and hold it over the button you want to replace. The button to be replaced gets a large white glow around it, and once you see that, you simply take your finger off the screen and your new button appears in that spot. That's all there is to it.

Using Maps to Find Just About Anything

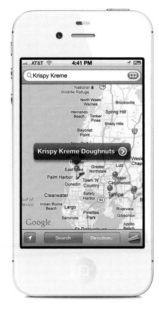

The Maps app lets you instantly find anything from the nearest golf course to a dry cleaner in the next city you're traveling to, and can not only give you precise directions on how to get there, it can call your destination, as well. Here's how to use it: Tap on the **Maps app** and when the Maps screen appears, you'll see a search field at the top where you can enter an address you'd like to see on the map. The iPhone will locate you on the map using the Location Services setting (go to the next page for more on this). Then it will find the location of the business that you search for that is closest to you. For example, let's say you'd like to find the nearest Krispy Kreme donut shop (not that I would actually ever search for one. Wink, wink). You'd tap once on the search field to bring up the keyboard, then you'd type in the name of the business, and tap the Search button. In the example shown above, I entered "Krispy Kreme," and on the Google map of my area, red pushpins appeared on the nearest locations. A little pop-up appears with the name of the location that is closest, and if you tap the blue arrow button in that pop-up, it takes you to an Info screen for that particular location. If you tap the phone number, it dials it for you (that way you could call and ask, "Is the Hot Now sign on?" Ya know, if you were so inclined). If you want to find a business that isn't near you, just add the city into the search. For example, typing "Krispy Kreme, Troy, Michigan" would locate the ones in, or close to, Troy, Michigan.

Locate Yourself on the Map

The iPhone uses cellular and Wi-Fi technology to find your location. If you have Location Services turned on in the General Settings, when you tap the Maps app, the iPhone will locate you on the map. If you have another map on your screen, just tap the **Locate Me button** at the bottom left of the screen (circled in red above). Once the iPhone knows where you are, Maps can then be used to search the surrounding area for the nearest businesses and services that you want to find. Just type "pizza" in the search field, tap Search, and Maps will locate all the local pizza joints close to your location.

---

iTip: Changing the Map Orientation

If you've located yourself in Maps, you can tap the Locate Me button once more to change the orientation of the map to the direction that you're facing.

Getting Driving Directions

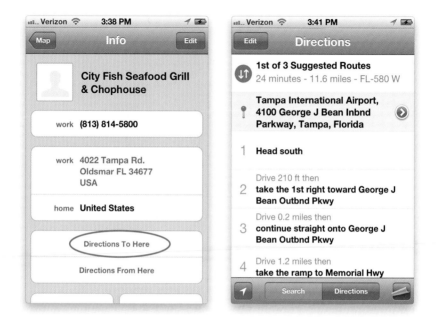

You can use the iPhone's Maps app to get step-by-step driving directions to any location and from any location. Let's say you want directions to your favorite restaurant—for me, it's City Fish Grill. Tap the Search button at the bottom of the Maps screen, then type in the name of the location you want to drive to—in my case, City Fish—and tap the Search button. Once it drops a pin on the map for the restaurant you want to drive to (if there is more than one pin, tap on the pin for the location you want), tap the little blue arrow button to the right of the pin's name. This will bring up the Info screen for the restaurant, including the phone number, so you can call and make reservations. Now tap the **Directions To Here button** on the Info screen, and this will take you to the Directions screen. To start from your current location, just tap the Route button, and the iPhone automatically figures out where you are and plots your route. If you want turn-by-turn directions, just tap the little curled page button at the bottom right of the Overview screen showing your route, and tap List. Because it has built-in GPS, the iPhone can track you along on your route as you drive.

iTip: Let Maps Find the Airport for You

Quick, what's the address of the nearest airport? You don't really have to know, because the Maps app has got you covered. All you need to know is the airport code (or just the name of the airport). For example, if you were trying to get to Chicago O'Hare International Airport, simply tap on the Maps app and type "ORD airport" into the search field. Tap the **Search button** *and the Maps app will zero right in on the airport's location.*

Drop a Pin on the Map

There will be times that you may not know the name of the business, or even the address, you're trying to get to. No problem! If you can find its general location on the map, you can use the Drop Pin feature to put a pin anywhere on the map you'd like. Once that pin is in place, you can use it as a reference point to get directions from where you are to the location that is marked by the pin. Tap on the Maps app, then get to the general vicinity that you want to go to on the map—you can do a search for a city, or a street, or anything else that's in the area. Then, tap the little curled page button in the lower-right corner of the screen to get to the other Maps options. Tap on **Drop Pin** to put a pin on the map, then you can move the pin around by just tapping on it and dragging it with your finger. Once the pin is in place, tap the pin, then tap the blue arrow button, and tap Directions To Here. This brings up the Directions screen, where you can tap the Route button at the bottom, and Maps will plot a route from where you are to where the pin is.

Display More Information on the Map

The Maps app can also show a satellite view and even the current traffic conditions. To get to these options, just tap the **curled page button** in the lower-right corner of any of the Maps screens. Tapping Standard shows you an illustrated map of the location that you search; Satellite will show you an actual satellite photo of the location you search; and Hybrid shows you the Satellite view with the street names—this is kind of the best of both worlds. Tapping List will show you turn-by-turn driving directions. The Show/Hide Traffic button adds real-time traffic flow info for the major highways (green for posted speed limit, yellow for below the posted speed limit, red for stop and go, and gray if there's no data).

Finding Your Contacts on the Map

You can search for your contacts in the Maps app if you have their street address in your contacts list. Let's say that you want to map a route to one of your contacts and call them before you head out. Well, you can do it all from the Maps app. When you start typing your contact's name in the search field, the Maps app starts searching through your contacts. Once you find the contact you want, just tap on it and Maps will locate their address on the map. Better yet, tap on the curled page button in the lower-right corner of the screen, then tap on the Satellite button, and it shows you a satellite photo of their house. To zoom in for a closer look, just double-tap on their location on the screen. If you want to call them, just tap the blue arrow button to the right of the pin, and you'll be taken to the contact's Info screen, which has the phone number (if you entered one). You can then just tap the phone number to dial it.

---

iTip: Switching from a List to a Map

*In the Maps app, if you're having the map give you directions from one location to another, and you're looking at the street-by-street, turn-by-turn List view of the directions, if you tap on **any of those directions**, it instantly switches back to Map view to pinpoint exactly where that list item appears on the map between the two locations.*

Build Up Your Contacts from the Maps App

If you look up a business by searching in the Maps app, and it's a business that you plan to continue to visit or call, why not have Maps add it to your contacts list? Tap on the Maps app and then search for the business you'd like to add. Once you find it, tap the blue arrow button to the right of the pin. On the Info screen that appears, scroll down and you'll see an **Add to Contacts button**. Tap it, then tap Create New Contact, and then tap Done, and this information will be added to your contacts list.

Use Map Bookmarks

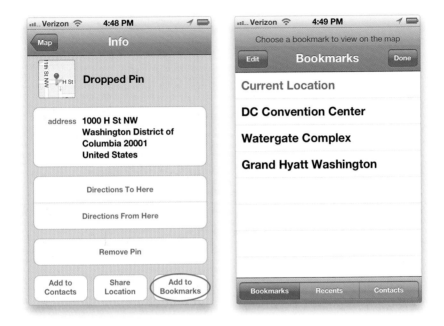

If you're traveling and you want to always be able to get back to the same place or have the same starting point (say your hotel) for each place you want to get a route to (or you get directions to places from home or work a lot), you can save your favorite locations as Bookmarks. You can create a Maps Bookmark from any of your search results or a dropped pin. Just tap the blue arrow button to the right of the pin's name and then tap **Add to Bookmarks**. You'll be able to name the Bookmark whatever you like. Then tap the Save button. Now, the next time you want directions to or from that location, you can use your Bookmark as a start or end destination in the Directions fields. Just tap Directions and then tap in either the Start or End field and you'll see a little Bookmarks button on the right (if the field already has a location in it, simply tap the little X at the right end of the field to clear it). Tap the Bookmarks button, then tap Bookmarks at the bottom to bring up your list of Bookmarks, then you can use any of them as a start or end point.

---

iTip: Finding a Recent Maps Search

The iPhone will also keep track of your most recent Maps searches, so even if you didn't bookmark a location that you recently searched for, it may still be in your Recents (tap the **Recents button** at the bottom of the Bookmarks screen) and accessible as a start or end point.

Seeing Your Local Weather

Tap on the **Weather app** and, in iOS 5, this brings up the local weather based on your location, without you having to actually add a new city. Also, now in iOS 5, tapping a weather screen will give you the detailed forecast for that day. By default, you'll also have a screen showing the weather in Cupertino, California, and if you swipe to the next screen, you'll see the weather forecast for New York. You can change these by tapping once on the little "i" button in the bottom right of the screen. This brings up the Weather screen, where you'll see Cupertino and New York listed with little red circular buttons in front of them. Tap on a button and then tap the Delete button that appears to the right to get rid of that city. To add your own city's weather, tap on the **+ (plus sign)** in the top-left corner and, using the keyboard at the bottom of the screen, type in your city and state, city and country, or zip code, then tap the Search button. It will then display your city in a list (if, of course, it finds your city), and all you have to do is tap on your city name, then tap the blue Done button in the upper-right corner.

---

iTip: How to Tell Day and Night in Weather

The color of the Weather screen lets you know whether it's day or night in the city you're looking at. If the Weather screen appears in blue, it's daytime, and if it's a dark purple, it's night.

Adding Appointments to Your Calendar

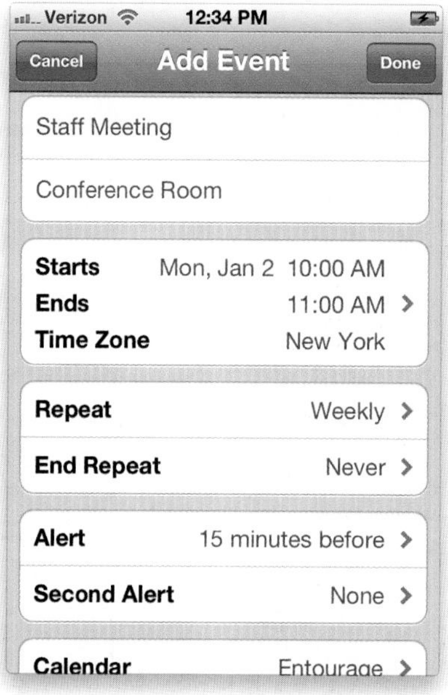

```
 .ıll Verizon 🛜        12:34 PM              🔋

 Cancel         Add Event          Done

 Staff Meeting

 Conference Room

 Starts        Mon, Jan 2   10:00 AM
 Ends                       11:00 AM  >
 Time Zone                  New York

 Repeat                      Weekly  >

 End Repeat                   Never  >

 Alert             15 minutes before  >

 Second Alert                 None  >

 Calendar                 Entourage  >
```

Tap on the Calendar app, then press the **+ (plus sign) button** in the upper-right corner of the Calendar screen to bring up the Add Event screen (as shown above). To give your event a name, tap on the Title field and the keyboard appears so you can type in a title (and a location, if you'd like). Tap on the Starts/Ends/Time Zone field to set the time when your event starts and ends, and the time zone it will be in. This brings up the Start & End screen, where you can choose the start time for your event by using the scroll wheels at the bottom of the screen. Then tap on Ends and choose the ending time. If this event runs the entire day, turn on the All-Day button by tapping on OFF. If you are traveling for the event, choose a time zone, as well. When you're done, tap the blue Done button. When you return to the Add Event screen, there are also options for repeating this event (for example, let's say you have a staff meeting every Monday at 10:00 a.m.—you can tap Repeat, and when the Repeat Event screen appears, you can choose Every Week, and it will add that event to your calendar every Monday at 10:00 a.m.). If you're using an iCloud, Microsoft Exchange, or CalDAV account, tap on Invitees to invite contacts. If you'd like to get a reminder alarm before your event, tap the Alert button. In the Event Alert screen, tap how long before the event you want the alarm to go off, then tap the Done button at the top of the screen (you can also add a second alarm). If you have multiple calendars, you can choose which calendar you want this event added to. You can also add a website or notes for your event. When everything's just the way you want it, tap the blue Done button in the top-right corner.

Subscribing to Calendars on Your iPhone

Not only can you sync your calendars to your iPhone, but you can also subscribe to calendars over the Internet right on your iPhone. For example, if your favorite sports team manages a calendar or your spouse publishes his/her iCal to iCloud, you can subscribe to those calendars directly. There are two ways to do this: The easy way would be for someone to email you the link to their calendar (iCal/ICS or CalDAV formats). Once you tap the link in the email, you'll get the option to subscribe to it. If you want to add one manually, you actually don't do it in the Calendar app at all. You go to your Settings app and then go to Mail, Contacts, Calendars. From there, you tap Add Account and then tap **Other**. From this screen, you can choose to add a CalDAV or Subscribed Calendar (ICS format).

Turn on the Birthday Calendar

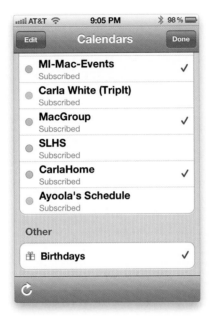

If you're good about adding people's birthdays to their contact info, you can use the built-in Birthdays calendar. This calendar will appear along with the rest of your calendars if it's turned on (tap on the Calendar app, then tap Calendars at the top left, and you'll see it under Other), and people's birthdays will automatically appear in it when you have their birthday in their contact info (from a contact's Info screen, tap Edit, then near the bottom, tap Add Field. Tap **Birthday**, enter the birthday from the scroll wheels, and tap Done). They will show up as all-day events that don't block your time. Sadly, there isn't a way to use this calendar to set reminders ahead of time. However, there are several third-party apps that will do that for you (for example, I like the one called Occasions).

Using the Built-In Voice Memos App

You launch the Voice Memos app from the Utilities folder on the Home screen and, whenever you're ready, you can tap the red **record button**. Once you've made your recording, press the same button to pause the recording or the button on the right to stop it. After you pause or stop the recording, if you press the button on the right, you can go to your list of recordings. From the list, you can play them back, delete them, or share them with others. Depending on your carrier's limits, you may have to trim a longer recording down before you can send it via email or messaging. Luckily, there's a trimming feature right in the Voice Memos app that will appear if the voice memo is too long to send. If it's not too long, but you still want to trim it, just tap the blue arrow button to the right of the voice memo in the list, then tap the Trim Memo button on the Info screen that appears. You can also sync the full length of the recording the next time you sync your iPhone with your computer—iTunes creates a special playlist of voice memos that get transferred from your iPhone.

Using the Compass

The iPhone comes with a built-in compass that is not just an app, but a real compass. From your Home screen, tap on the Utilities folder, then tap **Compass** and you'll be able to rotate your iPhone to see which direction you're headed in. If you tap the little "i" in the lower-right corner, you can toggle between Magnetic North and True North. This Compass feature also works in the Maps app to show you the direction you're headed in, if you have Location Services turned on. If you tap the Locate Me button in the bottom-left corner of the Compass screen, it will take you to the Maps app and the map will turn to show you the direction you are facing.

Nike + iPod

The iPhone has a built-in receiver for the Nike + iPod sensor for your running shoes. Since it already has the receiver, all you need to do is purchase the sensor and place it in a compatible pair of Nike shoes. Once the sensor is in place, you can adjust your preferences for Nike + iPod by going to the Settings app. The **Nike + iPod settings** will be in the bottom section, in your third-party application settings area. Once you've got it set, you can then launch the Nike + iPod app from your Home screen and choose your workout and playlist. The next time you sync your iPhone with iTunes, you'll have the option of uploading your results to the NikePlus.com website to track your progress.

Chapter 8

15 Useful Things to Ask Siri

Siri can do and answer lots of useful things that you probably wouldn't think to ask. So, here are a few things to try right off the bat:

- "Wake me at 7:30 a.m." (You can, of course, use whatever time you want.)
- "Call Terry." (Provided that you have a contact named Terry— you get the idea.)
- "Remind me to call Mom."
- "How do I get home?"
- "What time is it in London, England?"
- "What's 36 times 48?"
- "Play some Janet Jackson."
- "Set up a meeting at 10:00 a.m."
- "Tell Scott I'll call him later."
- "Email Bruce about the video."
- "I'm hungry."
- "Set a timer for 20 minutes."
- "Read my message."
- "Will it rain today?"
- "What does my calendar look like today?"

15 Fun Things to Ask Siri

SCOTT KELBY

While Siri is great at assisting you with day-to-day activities, she also has a sense of humor. So if you ask Siri a silly question, be prepared for a silly answer to come back. For some of these, there are multiple responses, so try it more than once to see what she says the next time. Here are a few to try:

- "I love you."
- "Beam me up."
- "Knock, knock."
- "How much wood can a woodchuck chuck?"
- "Tell me a joke."
- "Will you marry me?"
- "Where can I hide a body?"
- "What do you look like?"
- "What is your favorite color?"
- "Take a photo."
- "Hal, open the pod bay doors."
- "Who's your daddy?"
- "Call me an ambulance."
- "Are you conscious?"
- "Are you real?"

Using Siri Over Bluetooth or with Your Headset

TERRY WHITE

Siri's responses to you don't have to be heard by others. If you use a Bluetooth headset or the supplied Apple wired headset, you can use Siri more privately. If you're using a compatible Bluetooth headset, just press-and-hold the talk/answer button on it for a few moments until you hear the Siri beep, or it may say "voice dialing." Then you can speak your command to Siri and hear it back in your earpiece. With the Apple earbuds, just pinch the center of the headset button for a few moments and Siri should activate. If your car has Bluetooth and you've paired your iPhone 4S with it, Siri may work there, too. In my car, if I hold down the Home button on my iPhone 4S, my car stereo will pause and my voice commands and responses will be played through the car's speakers. It doesn't work with all car Bluetooth systems, but give it a try.

Tips for Better Results with Siri

Siri does a great job out of the box. However, you can get even better results if you ask her things in a better way. Sometimes it's easy for Siri to get confused by the way you ask the question. For example, if you say, "Tell my sister Willie Blue is coming for dinner," Siri will probably respond, "Okay, do you want me to remember Willie Blue is your sister?" Instead, ask Siri to "Tell my sister *that* Willie Blue is coming for dinner." Also, when you have names of relatives that may be hard for Siri to understand, it might be easier to add the relative as a "relationship" in your contact info. That way, instead of asking Siri to call a specific name, you can simply say, "Call my father."

A few more cool things to ask Siri:

- "What is the tip on $25.51?"
- "How much is $15.21 plus Michigan sales tax?"
- "Yahoo, Detroit Lions score!" (Great for games in-progress or the last game played.)
- "Remind me to call home when I leave here." (This will set up a location-based reminder.)

Post to Twitter with Siri

As of the writing of this book, Siri can't tweet for you, but there is a workaround: First, you'll need to go to your Contacts app and create a new contact with "Twitter" as the first name and "404-04" as the phone number. Next, send a text message to that number with the word "Start." You'll get a reply asking for your Twitter username (or for you to sign up), then a reply asking for your password, then finally a reply asking you to confirm that you want to use Twitter on your iPhone. Once you send that last reply, SMS will be enabled on your Twitter account. Now, you can just say to Siri, "Tell Twitter [whatever you want your tweet to be]," and Siri will send a text message to your Twitter contact, which will send your tweet to your Twitter page.

Add to Your Grocery List with Siri

While there are some great grocery list apps for iOS 5 in the App Store, as of the writing of this book, there aren't any that are voice-activated yet. Therefore, you might appreciate this tip on getting Siri to add to your grocery list for you. The first thing you'll need to do is go to the Reminders app and create a new List called "Grocery" (tap on the Lists button near the top left, then tap the Edit button in the top right, tap Create New List to create your new list, then tap the Done button). Now that you have a Reminder list called "Grocery," you can add to this list anytime you want by bringing Siri up and saying something like, "Add bread to the Grocery list," and Siri will create this reminder for you and ask you to confirm it.

Chapter Nine

McCloud

Keep Everything in Sync Using iCloud

 If you just read that chapter title, "McCloud," and thought that was a reference to something on the menu at McDonald's, then you clearly weren't around back in 1970 when NBC aired a groundbreaking TV series about Marshal Sam McCloud (played by actor Dennis Weaver)—who was a lawman from out west on temporary assignment with the New York City Police Department, who were kept pretty darn busy back then, because in 1970 they had no simple, reliable way to keep their music, movies, and calendars on their iPhones, iPod touches, and iPads all in sync. I remember this one episode where McCloud (on the show they usually just called him "McCloud," rather than by his rap name "Sa-dizzle") was busting these two thugs at West 44th and Broadway, when one of the guys reaches in his jacket pocket to pull out what McCloud thinks must be a gun. So, he dives behind a Ford Pinto Wagon to take cover, but the guy actually pulls out his iPhone instead. Well, of course, McCloud is relieved but takes the iPhone from the thug and starts looking at his Calendar app to see if this guy has any appointments for illegal drug pickups or selling black market 8-track tapes or any of that New York street thug stuff. But, then it hits him—McCloud realizes that the guy just hasn't synced his phone in a while. So, he goes to Crazy Eddie's to buy a sync cable, but the clerk at the counter (played by Buddy Hackett) can't find one anywhere (it's a hilarious scene). So, McCloud has to let the punk go, but as he's handing the thug back his iPhone, a 1971 Datsun B210 careens around the corner, and its side mirror knocks the iPhone out of his hand, and it lands in the street and is crushed by a Ford Galaxie 500 trailing right behind him. McCloud realizes that now we'll never know if the guy was guilty, so he just shoots him. Man, now that was a show!

iCloud Settings

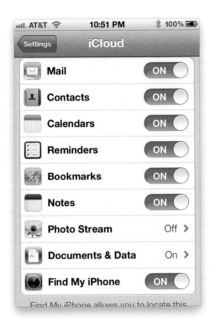

Apple transitioned its online service from MobileMe to iCloud (you can move your MobileMe to iCloud at www.me.com/move). iCloud allows you to sync your Mail, Contacts, Calendars, Reminders, Bookmarks, Notes, Photos, and documents, as well as back up your iPhone's data. Unlike MobileMe, iCloud is *free*. Once you set up your Apple ID on iCloud, you can go to your iPhone's Settings app and tap iCloud. You can choose which kinds of data you want synced (or not) by turning them on (or off) individually. Until now, your iPhone has backed up to your computer each time you plugged it in and synced (if you had that preference set). Now you have the option of turning on the iCloud backup—your iPhone will back up to iCloud each time you plug it in to a power source and you're on Wi-Fi. The advantage is that you can do a restore from anywhere that you have Wi-Fi, in case you have a problem or emergency. Under Storage & Backup, on the iCloud screen, you can also see your available storage (you get 5 GB) or purchase more storage.

---

iTip: Restore from an iCloud Backup

*If something happens to your iPhone and you need to restore it (or a new one) from your iCloud backup, in the Setup Assistant, tap **Restore from iCloud Backup**. Enter your Apple ID and Password, and choose which of the three most recent backups you want to use. Your iPhone will restart, your accounts and data will be restored, and your iTunes Store purchases will start downloading.*

Your Data in the iCloud

The most common use for iCloud syncing is data, like Mail, Contacts, Calendar, Reminders, Bookmarks, and Notes. The advantage of using iCloud to sync this data is that you can update it on your computer or your iPhone and it will update in the other place over the air. You can also edit or view your data at www.iCloud.com. If you're on a Mac running Mac OS X 10.7 Lion or greater, the built-in applications like Address Book, iCal, Safari, and Mail support iCloud syncing. It works well and it's very seamless. If you're on a Windows PC, you can use Outlook 2007 or 2010 and an up-to-date version of your Web browser. Apple makes an iCloud Control Panel for Windows Vista and Windows 7. You can download it at: www.apple.com/icloud/setup/pc.html.

Your Music in the iCloud

There are two ways to enjoy your music via iCloud. Just by having iCloud and an Apple ID, you can always access your purchased music (or books, or TV shows) from the iTunes Store. Apple allows you to re-download any of your purchases. However, if you go with an iTunes Match account, you not only get access to your iTunes Store Purchased music, but also to all of your music that's been synced to iCloud from your Mac or PC. Yes, even songs that you didn't buy from iTunes. You sign up for iTunes Match in iTunes, and once the process is complete, you can turn it on, on your iPhone. This will wipe any existing music from your iPhone and give you access to all of your playlists and songs. The cost of iTunes Match is $24.99 per year.

Your Photos in the iCloud

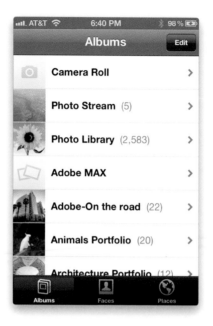

iCloud includes the ability to sync your 1,000 most recent photos between your iPhone, computer, and the iCloud website. Once you turn it on, any photos you take with your iPhone camera will automatically be uploaded to iCloud. If your Mac is running iPhoto 9.2 or higher or Aperture 3.2 or higher, you have Apple TV, or have a Windows PC (with the iCloud Control Panel installed) Pictures Library, and you add photos to any of these sources, they'll appear in the Photo Stream area of your iPhone, too. While this is great, there are some things to note in this initial implementation. First, Photo Stream is all or nothing. You can't pick and choose which photos to sync with it. It will sync your 1,000 most recent photos, or any photo less than 30 days old. You can't delete a photo from your Photo Stream without deleting it from your iPhone, too. As long as you're willing to live with these limitations, then Photo Stream is great.

Your Documents in the iCloud

iCloud lets you sync documents, too. This means that if you're using Apple's iWork apps (Pages, Numbers, or Keynote), then you can have those documents sync with iCloud. This also means that if you create a Pages document on your iPhone, you could continue editing it on your iPad. As of the writing of this book, you can't sync iWork '09 documents directly with iCloud on the Mac, but you can download iCloud documents from the iCloud website to work on in your Mac version of iWork, or as Microsoft office documents or PDFs. I imagine that the next version of iWork will have this support built-in to make the iCloud documents story complete.

Backing Up to iCloud

Until now, you've only been able to back up your iPhone via iTunes on your Mac or PC. Now, with iCloud, you can turn on an iCloud backup in the Settings app, and when your iPhone is plugged into a power source, is on Wi-Fi, and is locked, it will back up wirelessly to iCloud. You may be wondering what the advantage is of doing it via iCloud vs. your computer, and there really aren't a ton of advantages. One is that it will mean taking up less space on your computer's hard drive. The other, and probably more serious, advantage is that by backing up to iCloud, if your iPhone is ever lost or stolen while you're on the road, you'd be able to replace it with a new one and restore wirelessly from iCloud without having to have your computer with you.

---

iTip: Initiate a Manual Backup to iCloud

*Although your iPhone will back up automatically to iCloud when you plug it into a power source, and it's locked and on WiFi, you can initiate a manual backup whenever you want just by going to the bottom of the iCloud settings, tapping Storage & Backup, and then tapping the **Back Up Now button**.*

Chapter Ten

The Song Remains the Same

Using iTunes and the iTunes Store

 Any chapter that is named after a Led Zeppelin movie from 1976 has to get some special credit in rock 'n' roll heaven, right? This is another movie I never saw, but I'm pretty sure it had Jimmy Stewart and Ann Margaret in it at some point. Didn't it? Anyway, this chapter is about how to use iTunes and the iTunes Store (which used to be called the iTunes Music Store until Apple added TV shows, movies, and the App Store, and then it seemed silly to still call it a music store, especially when it had huge hit movies in it like *Star Trek: The Wrath of Khan* [that was with Leonardo DiCaprio and Ellen DeGeneres, wasn't it?] and *Zoolander* [with Meryl Streep and David Niven, I believe]). Anyway, here's the thing: in this chapter I will endeavor to help those who (a) have never had an iPod, and thus (b) never used iTunes, which means you've (c) never been to the iTunes Store, which means (d) you're not a teen, because every person between the ages of 13 and 19 has to report to the iTunes Store as part of the government's Selective Service Online Shopping Act of 1984, which stipulates that every male child over the age of 14 must stare directly and blankly into a hand-held video game device for no less than nine hours per day (including a mandatory two hours during school). As I was saying, this chapter is for people who need a quick course on what iTunes is, what's in the iTunes Store (and how to buy stuff there), and then how to get that stuff into their iPhone without any person between the ages of 13 and 19 ever looking up from their screen. This, I think we can do.

Buying Songs on Your Computer

You buy music for your iPhone from the iTunes Store and to enter the store, just click on iTunes Store in the Source list on the left side of the iTunes window. Although you can jump directly to different genres (like Rock, Hip-Hop/Rap, Country, Pop, etc.) and browse through there, the quickest way to find the music you want is to do a search using the Search Store field in the upper-right corner of the iTunes window. Here I entered "Jay-Z," then hit the Return (PC: Enter) key on my keyboard, and in just seconds all the Jay-Z albums and songs available in iTunes appeared (as seen here). You can buy (and down-load on the spot) individual songs for 69¢, 99¢, or $1.29, or an entire album for varying prices (Jay-Z albums go for anywhere from $5.99 to $19.99). To hear a 90-second preview of any song, double-click on its title. If you want to buy a song, click the **Buy button** (circled above in red), and it's immediately downloaded to your computer (of course, before you can start buying and downloading songs, you'll have to take a moment to create an iTunes account). Okay, so that's pretty much the scoop—you can use the Search Store field to find just the song(s) you want, or you can click the Home button (that little icon that looks like a house, at the top of the iTunes Store window), and browse through the iTunes Store's huge collection of songs (there are more than 10 million songs in the iTunes Store). Any songs you buy are added to your Music Library, and they'll also appear under Purchased in the Source list.

Importing Songs from CDs

Chances are if you haven't been using an MP3 player (like an iPod) up to this point, most of your music collection is still on CDs. Luckily, getting them into iTunes (and from there into your iPhone) couldn't be easier. Start by launching iTunes. When iTunes appears, put a music CD into your computer's CD/DVD drive, and a dialog will appear asking if you'd like to import the songs on your CD into your iTunes Music Library. All you have to do is click the Yes button, and iTunes does the rest—importing each song, in order, with the track names—for you. It puts these songs into your Music Library mixed in with all your other songs (see "Creating Music Playlists" on page 185 for how to keep these songs separate).

---

iTip: iTunes Will Add the Track Names

If you have an Internet connection when you go to import a music CD, iTunes will go to the Web, cross reference the name of your CD with an online music database, and in most cases, it will automatically add the track names to all of your songs. If it couldn't find your CD in its vast database, you must have some mighty obscure musical taste, and I mean that in the most nonjudgmental, totally disingenuous way possible.

Using Parental Controls to Protect Your Kids

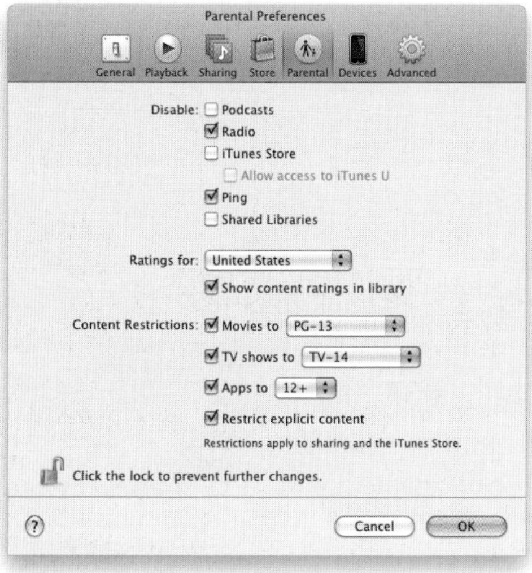

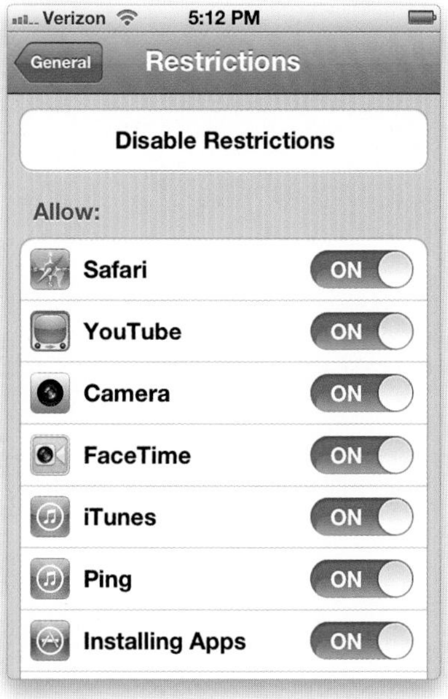

Both iTunes and your iPhone have built-in parental controls with a wide range of settings you can use to protect your kids from downloading movies, apps, or songs you'd prefer they didn't download. Luckily, it's not just a Yes/No proposition, because there are options for choosing the ratings of the movies they can download from the iTunes Store, and whether they can download songs with explicit lyrics or not. In iTunes, press **Command-,** (comma; **PC: Ctrl-,**) to open the Preferences dialog, and click on Parental at the top. After you choose your settings, be sure to click the Lock icon in the bottom left to keep your kids from changing them. On your iPhone, you turn this feature on (and choose your personal options and password) by tapping on the Settings app, then tapping on General, and tapping on Restrictions. Now tap on the **Enable Restrictions button** at the top. After you set a passcode, a list of things you can restrict appears below what is now the Disable Restrictions button. By default, it restricts everything (installing apps, buying movies, you name it). To turn off a restriction, just tap on the ON button next to it. Scroll down further for a list of Allowed Content options, where you can set ratings for things they purchase.

Creating Music Playlists

The way you keep things organized in your Music Library is by creating playlists, which are basically collections of your favorite songs. So, for example, if you wanted to create a collection of nothing but your favorite songs to listen to in the car, you would start by clicking on the **+ (plus sign) button** at the bottom-left corner of the iTunes window. This adds a new blank playlist to your Source list, and its name is highlighted so you can type in a name (how about "Scott's Driving Tunes"?). Once you've named your playlist, press the Return (PC: Enter) key on your keyboard to lock in the name of your playlist, then make sure you click on Music in the Source list to show your entire iTunes Music Library of songs. Now, scroll through your music collection and each time you run across one of your favorite driving songs, click-and-drag that song onto your Driving Tunes playlist in the Source list. A green circle with a + (plus sign) in it appears to let you know that you're adding a song to that playlist (as seen here). Once you've gone through and added all your driving favorites, you're only one click away from hearing just those songs (and you'll be able to transfer this new playlist to your iPhone). Also, once your songs are in a playlist, you can click-and-drag them into the order you'd like them to appear. To delete a song from a playlist, just click on it and hit the Delete (PC: Backspace) key on your keyboard (this doesn't delete it from your Music Library, just from that playlist).

Creating Smart Playlists

Smart Playlist

☑ Match the following rule:

(Artist ⬍) (contains ⬍) [Foo Fighters]　　　　　　　　⊕

☐ Limit to [25] [items ⬍] selected by [random ⬍]
☐ Match only checked items
☑ Live updating

(?)　　　　　　　　　(Cancel) (OK)

If you don't want to take the time to make a bunch of different playlists (actually, making your own custom playlists is half the fun of using iTunes), you can have iTunes do most of the work for you. iTunes already comes with some of these "Smart Playlists." For example, you'll see playlists already created with the 25 songs you've played the most, the songs you've played most recently, and if you rate your songs in iTunes (using the 1- to 5-star rating system), you'll see only your top-rated songs in a Smart Playlist. To create your own Smart Playlist, just press-and-hold the **Option key** on a Mac, or the **Shift key** on a PC, and click the **+ (plus sign) button** at the bottom-left corner of iTunes (it changes to look like a gear). This brings up a dialog that asks you to choose the criteria for your new Smart Playlist. So, let's say you've imported three or four different Foo Fighters CDs, and you've bought some Foo Fighters songs from the iTunes Store. When the Smart Playlist dialog appears, you can have it search your entire Music Library and build a playlist of all your Foo Fighters songs for you (as shown above). These Smart Playlists are incredibly powerful, yet easy to use—you just choose your criteria from the pop-up menus. Let's try another: want all of your country songs in one playlist? Change the Artist field to Genre, erase "Foo Fighters" and type in "Country," then click OK. To narrow your criteria even further, click the gray + (plus sign) button to the right of the text field (where you typed "Country") to add another line of search criteria.

Creating Genius Playlists in iTunes

iTunes includes an incredible feature that creates a playlist based on one song you choose and other songs you have in your Music Library that are similar or would go well with it. Choose **Turn On Genius** from the Store menu, and iTunes will send an anonymous snapshot of your Music Library up to "the clouds" (Apple's iTunes servers), where it will be combined with Music Library lists from other users to create more accurate Genius playlists based on the songs you choose. Once you have the Genius feature turned on, all you have to do is choose a song in your Music Library, click the **Genius button** in the bottom right-hand corner, and iTunes will build a new playlist of up to 25 songs that should go well with the song you initially selected. You can choose between 25, 50, 75, and 100 songs from the Limit To pop-up menu at the top of the main iTunes window. You can also click the Save Playlist button at the top if you want to keep it and use it again in the future, or click the Refresh button to see if the Genius feature makes an even better playlist (this will be more helpful if you save the playlist and refresh it later, after you've added more songs and Apple has gathered more information). By default, your iTunes Genius information will be updated weekly, so that your Genius playlists get even smarter.

Downloading Podcasts in iTunes

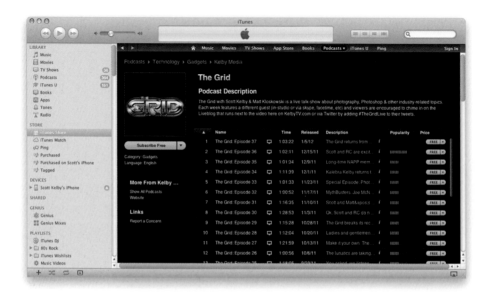

Podcasts are free audio or video shows produced by individuals or companies on a wide range of topics, from teaching you how to cook, to teaching you martial arts, to shows that are just comedy, or product reviews, or news. Everyone from ESPN to National Geographic, from HBO to NPR (radio), and about everybody in between offers free downloadable podcasts, which you can subscribe to (for free) and they're down-loaded to your computer (and then onto your iPhone, if you choose) as soon as each episode is released (some are daily, some post weekly episodes, some bi-weekly, etc.). To find a podcast you'd like, go to the iTunes Store, and on the homepage click on Pod-casts. On the Podcasts main page, you can search through different categories (like Sports & Recreation, Technology, Business, etc.). When you find one you like, you can click the **Free button** to download just an episode, or click the **Subscribe Free button** to download each episode for free as they're released (you can unsubscribe any time).

> **iTip: Scott's and Terry's Video Podcasts**
>
> *Terry and I both do weekly video podcasts. Mine (Scott's) are called* The Grid *and Photo-shop User TV (www.kelbytv.com) and Terry's is the* Adobe Creative Suite Podcast *(www.creativesuitepodcast.com). You can subscribe to these podcasts for free right from within iTunes on your computer, or download them right on your iPhone.*

Buying or Renting Videos in iTunes

From the iTunes Store homepage, in the navigation bar at the top of the main window, click on either Movies or TV Shows (you'll find music videos under Music). When your choice appears, you'll find featured titles. For example, if you chose TV Shows, you would see the entire seasons of TV shows from ABC, NBC, CBS, FOX, and more than 110 broadcast and cable channels (individual episodes cost $1.99 each, but you can buy an entire season of a show—every episode which aired that year—and those prices vary. You can also buy high-definition versions of many shows—they cost $2.99). Movies have their own section in the iTunes Store, as well, and full-length movies run from around $9.99 to $14.99, for the most part. Some are available in high-definition (HD) for up to $19.99. You can also rent movies for $2.99 and $3.99 ($4.99 for HD), and you'll have 30 days to enjoy them either on your iPhone, iPad, iPod, computer, or Apple TV. Once you start watching a movie rental, you'll have 24 hours to finish it or watch it as many times as you like before it deletes itself.

iTip: Creating Video Playlists

Playlists aren't just for music—you can create your own custom playlists for your favorite TV shows or movies (so you could have a playlist of just scary movies, or a playlist of classic TV shows). You create them just like you would a music playlist.

189

Choosing What Goes into Your iPhone

Since iPhones don't have as much storage space as your computer does, iTunes lets you choose which music playlists, TV shows, etc., get uploaded. To do this, connect your iPhone to your computer and then in iTunes, click on your iPhone in the Source list on the left to bring up its preferences. Along the top of the window, you'll see Music, Photos, Movies, etc. For example, click on TV Shows and when those preferences appear, turn on the Sync TV Shows checkbox and then choose the shows you want uploaded to your iPhone. You can choose to upload all unwatched shows, or just the three most recent, five most recent, etc. You can control which shows, and how many, are uploaded to your iPhone. When you're done, click the **Apply button** in the lower-right corner. To sync your rented movies (at the top of the Movies tab), click on the Move button next to each rented movie you want on your iPhone, then click the Apply button. Your computer needs to be connected to the Internet when you do the sync and once you sync your rental(s) to your iPhone, it is removed from your computer's iTunes Movies Library.

---

iTip: Where to Find More Info on iTunes

We've just scratched the surface of what you can do in iTunes and the iTunes Store. If you're into this kind of stuff, we know a guy who wrote a killer book on iTunes, the iPod, and the iTunes Store. His book is called (ready for this?) The iPod Book (from Peachpit Press), and we have to say, it looks pretty much like this book. In fact, this book is based on the layout and design of that book. But we won't get in trouble because Scott's the author of that book, too! (Aw come on, you knew that was coming, right?)

Turn On Automatic Downloads

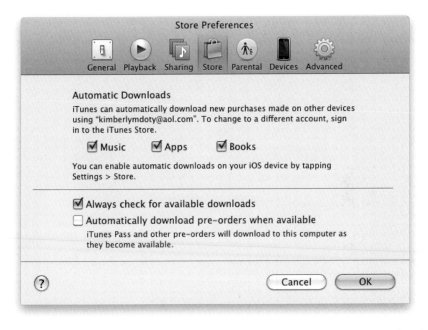

When you make a purchase in the iTunes Store on your computer, certain content (music, apps, and books) can be automatically downloaded to your iPhone, iPad, or iPod touch using the Automatic Download feature. You can find the Automatic Download settings by clicking on Purchased in the iTunes Source List and then clicking on **Configure Automatic Downloads** at the bottom of the window (you need to sign in to the iTunes Store first). You can turn the individual settings on or off for Music, Apps, or Books. If they're on, when you buy or download content on your computer that content is automatically downloaded to your devices. (*Note:* If you buy music, apps, or books on your devices, and you want them to automatically download to your computer, you'll have to turn Automatic Downloading on in the Store settings on your device.) This is pretty sweet as it means that in most cases you won't have to sync just to get new stuff that you downloaded. Also, if you're purchasing large files or if you have a limited data plan, then you probably want to turn off Use Cellular Data in your iPhone's Store settings.

Chapter Eleven

I Got the Music in Me

Using Your iPhone's Built-In iPod That's Not Called an iPod

 "Ain't got no trouble in my life. No foolish dream to make me cry." These are the opening lines to KiKi Dee's hit song "I Got the Music in Me," and before we get on to the business of not really talking about the iPod in your iPhone, let's break this down for a moment, because those two opening lines beg more questions than they answer. First, if you're wondering "Who is Kiki Dee?" then we can establish that you do know who Bruno Mars is, which means Kiki Dee is officially old enough to be your mother. *Update:* I just checked and she's now 65 years old, so she could actually be your grandmother, but if your mom was pretty frisky at a young age and had you when she was just out of school, then Kiki Dee could actually be your great grandmother, and if that's the case, you need to give her a call and have a little talk about: (a) Her grammar, which frankly is appalling. "Ain't got no…"? Really? *"Ain't got no"*? Wasn't grammar like a big deal back in the days when she was churning butter with a hand-turned paddle? Anyway, while you've got her on the phone, also ask her (b) why your mom (her granddaughter) was so promiscuous at such an early age, and (c) where she got the name Kiki Dee when her given name was Pauline Matthews [true] or Stella Ludmakker (I made that one up, but if she had been named Stella Ludmakker, she wouldn't have needed a stage name). Anyway, as you can see, this whole Kiki Dee thing opens up a can of worms that I fear could derail the whole purpose of this chapter intro, which is to prepare you to learn how to use your iPhone's built-in iPod that Apple doesn't call an iPod, because they separated the music and video parts into two separate apps, much like your great grandmother once separated the cream from rich whole milk to make what you kids today call "butter," which, not coincidentally, would make a great name for an app about breakfast or *French Cooking with Mademoiselle Kiki Dee.*

Setting Up Your iTunes Library to Sync with Your iPhone

To get the music, movies, etc., from your iTunes Library on your computer onto your iPhone, just connect your iPhone to your computer using the USB cable that came with it, and once you set some preferences, it will transfer your music, playlists, movies, and so on, right over to your iPhone (this can also be done wirelessly, as you'll learn on the next page). However, you probably do want some control over how this is done, because your computer has a lot more storage space than your iPhone does, and if you have thousands of songs, and hundreds of movies and TV shows, they may not all fit. Luckily, you can choose exactly which songs, playlists, movies, TV shows, podcasts, etc., actually do get transferred over to your iPhone using the little tabs that appear across the top of the main iTunes window when you click on your iPhone in the Devices list on the left side of the window. Take a look at the Music preferences above. When you turn on the Sync Music checkbox, by default, it wants to move all your music over to your iPhone, but if you click the Selected Playlists, Artists, Albums, and Genres radio button, you can choose which songs are copied over (only the ones you turn on a checkbox for will get copied over). You can do this for podcasts, movies, TV shows—you name it. Once you make your choices, click the **Apply button** in the lower-right corner. If you have music and videos on more than one computer, such as a laptop and desktop, then you'll want to manually drag them onto your iPhone instead of syncing them. To do this, connect your iPhone to your computer and click on it in the Devices list on the left side of iTunes. On the Summary tab, turn on the checkbox for **Manually Manage Music and Videos**.

Don't Plug In—Now You Can Sync Wirelessly

In the past, when it was time to sync the music on your computer with the music on your iPhone, there was really only one way to do it—get out the white sync/charging USB cable that came with your iPhone, connect your iPhone to your computer, and then let iTunes sync them. Well, now, at long last, we have the dream—wireless syncing. All you have to do is turn it on (you do have to do one last "connect your iPhone to your computer" to set this up, but once you do, it sets you free from there on out). So, start by connecting your iPhone to your computer using that white sync USB cable. Launch iTunes, and click on your iPhone in the Devices list on the left side of the window, then click on the Summary tab in the main window (if it's not already showing). Near the bottom, turn on the **Sync with this iPhone over Wi-Fi checkbox** and then click the Apply button on the bottom right. Okay, that's it for the computer side of things. Now you have to turn it on, on your iPhone. So, tap on the Settings app, then tap on General, and then tap on **iTunes Wi-Fi Sync**. Make sure the computer you just turned on wireless syncing for is showing below the Sync Now button, then tap the **Sync Now button** and you have just joined the space age wireless "developed by NASA for the Space Shuttle Program (not really)" world of wireless syncing. Cut the cord, baby! (Of course, don't really cut the cord—you still need it to charge your iPhone.)

Playing Music on Your iPhone

Once you have music imported into your iPhone, you play your music with the **Music app** (I know, it seems kinda obvious). At the bottom of the Music app's screen, tap the Playlists, Artists, or Songs button (or Genius, if you have that feature turned on in iTunes) to find the first song that you want to hear. Once you find the song, just tap it to begin playing it. If you don't have your headset plugged in, you'll actually hear the music through your iPhone's built-in speaker. If the song has album art, you'll see that while the song plays (if there is no album art, then it just displays a default music note). The song's title, album, and artist appear at the top of the screen. Once your song finishes, it plays the next song in the list. To conserve battery life, after a little while your iPhone's display will go to sleep, but don't worry, the song will keep playing. To get back to the Music app, just press the Home button and unlock the iPhone by swiping your finger across to the right on the Slide to Unlock button. *Note:* Although you launch the Music app to choose which playlist or songs you want to listen to, once you actually start a song, podcast, or audiobook playing, you can then switch over to and start using other apps, or play games, or whatever, and your music (or audiobook, podcast, etc.) keeps playing.

Buying Songs on Your iPhone

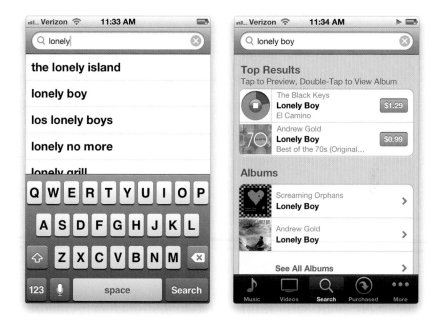

Apple's iTunes Store is the biggest music store in the world, with millions of songs to choose from, and buying songs there is simple. Launch the iTunes app, and its homepage shows you the latest releases. Of course, there's a top-10 list by genre, or you can browse by genre, but if you know the song you're trying to find, just tap the Search button (at the bottom center of the screen). Now, type in either the name of the song you're looking for, or the band or album name—whatever ya got that will lead you to the song you want. When your search results appear, you can listen to a 90-second preview of the song (to make sure it's the version of the song you want) by tapping once on the song. Then, if you want to buy that song, you can just tap the price button (at the time this book was published, songs on the iTunes Store cost 69¢, 99¢, or $1.29 US), then tap the **Buy Song button**. It's going to ask you for your Apple ID (to make sure it's you), and then the song downloads. It's normally a very quick download, since it's just a small audio file. To hear the song you just bought, go to your Music app, tap on Playlists, then tap on Purchased, and the last song at the bottom of the list is the one you just bought. To hear it, just tap on it.

Using iTunes Match to Back Up Your Other Songs to iCloud

When you turn on Apple's iCloud feature on your iPhone (see Chapter 9), turn on the iCloud backup, and run your first backup, it automatically backs up any music, books, or TV shows you've bought from the iTunes Store wirelessly to iCloud. However, it doesn't back up music you imported from CDs or bought somewhere else, but for around $25 a year, Apple offers a service called "iTunes Match." It searches your Music Library, finds which songs there are available in the iTunes Store, and when it finds a match, it adds it to your iCloud backup. So, what if it can't find some of your songs? (Hey, it could happen. Especially if some of your songs are from the Partridge Family. Kidding. I hope.) Then, you just upload those to iCloud yourself, and you're fully backed up. But it's not just the backing up of your songs that rocks about this—once it's set up, you can now stream your entire Music Library to any of your devices, so you always have access to it (and when it plays back, if the quality of your upload wasn't pristine, it streams it at high-quality 256-Kbps AAC quality). How sweet is that? (I signed up for this as soon as it came out, and I love it!).

> **iTip: Downloading Old iTunes Store Purchases from iCloud**
>
> When you turn on iCloud on your iPhone, it backs up not only your iTunes Store purchases made on your iPhone, but also any purchases made on your computer or other devices. You can see all of your purchases or just the ones not on your iPhone by tapping **Purchased** in the iTunes app. If a song (or book, or TV show) is not on your iPhone, you can download it from iCloud by tapping on the little cloud icon with a down-facing arrow that's next to the song (book, TV show) title.

Stream Music Wirelessly to Your Stereo Using AirPlay

All you need is either an AirPlay-compatible audio system (lots of companies make these, including JBL, Pioneer, Phillips, iHome, and B&W among others) or an Apple TV (it's not actually a television set, it's a very cool accessory you attach to your TV that lets you buy and rent movies and television shows, and a whole lot more), and then you're one tap away from streaming the music on your iPhone to your audio system. Here's how to use your iPhone's AirPlay feature: when you're playing a song, you'll see a button to the right of your Fast Forward button (its icon looks like a widescreen TV with a triangle at the bottom); tap on that button and a list of any AirPlay-compatible speakers or Apple TVs you have connected appears. Tap on the set of speakers (or Apple TV) you want to have your music streamed to, and it starts streaming to those speakers (of course, you have to have the power on, on your AirPlay speaker system or Apple TV and home entertainment system, but you figured that, right?).

---

iTip: Controlling Your AirPlay Music Using Apple's Remote App

You can also use AirPlay to stream music wirelessly directly from iTunes on your computer, and if you're going to do that, you'll want to download Apple's free Remote iPhone app. It's like a remote control for your AirPlay devices right on your iPhone, so you can change songs, mute the sound, choose different AirPlay speakers, skip a song—you name it. You can find it in the App Store.

Seeing Your List of Songs

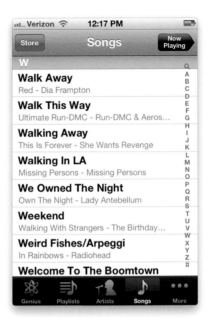

When you launch the Music app, at the bottom of the screen you will have buttons that will take you directly to your Genius mixes, playlists, or a listing of artists or songs. There's also a More button to take you to other categories like Albums, Audiobooks, Podcasts, etc. To find a song, just tap the **Songs button** at the bottom of the screen and you'll get an alphabetical list of all the songs in your iPhone's Music app (the songs are listed by title, but the album and artist are listed below each song). If you want to jump to a particular letter in the alphabet, just tap on that letter in the list of letters running down the right side of the screen, and it jumps to songs that begin with that letter. (*Note:* You can also just slide your finger up/down this list and the song list will scroll up/down the alphabet right along with you.) When you find a song you want to hear, just tap on it, and that song's screen appears, and it starts playing.

---

iTip: Seeing Your Song Count

*If you want to see how many songs you have on your iPhone, tap the **Songs button** and scroll down to the bottom of the list. You can see your song count listed there.*

Searching for Songs

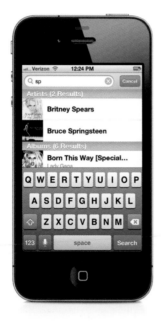

If you've got hundreds, or even thousands, of songs in your iPhone's Music app, you're gonna love the built-in Spotlight search feature (you just have to know where to find it, because it's not that obvious at first). For example, if you want to search your song list, in the Music app, tap on Songs at the bottom of the screen, then flick downward on the screen. A **Search field** appears at the top of the screen. Tap in the field, and the keyboard will appear. Just start typing in the name of the song, or artist, you want to listen to, and as soon as you start typing just a few letters, the results appear onscreen. There is the system-wide Spotlight search feature (which you get to by flicking to the right from your first Home screen) that searches everything on your iPhone, but by going to the Music app first and tapping Songs, it just searches your song list, so it's easier to get right to the song you want.

Play/Pause, Skipping Songs, Rewind & Volume

To play any song, just tap on it and it starts playing. To pause the song, tap the Pause button (it looks like two vertical lines), which appears at the bottom center of the screen when you're playing a song. Once you've paused a song, that Pause button turns into a Play button (it looks like a right-facing triangle). You can jump to the next song by tapping the right-facing double arrows next to the Play/Pause button. To jump back to the beginning of the current song, tap the left-facing double arrows once, and to jump back to the previous song, tap the left-facing double arrows twice. If you want to fast-forward through a song, tap-and-hold the right-facing double arrows. To rewind, tap-and-hold the left-facing double arrows. If you're wearing the earbuds (headset) that came with your iPhone, there is a little microphone right on the cable, but it's also a button—to pause the current song, press it once; to jump to the next song, press it twice quickly. If your iPhone is locked and you want to pause the music for a moment, just press the Home button twice, then tap the Pause button that appears near the top of the screen. As for volume, there are two ways to adjust it: Use the onscreen volume slider that is at the bottom of the Music app screen—just tap-and-drag the knob (circle) to the right to make the volume louder, or to the left to lower it. The other way is to use the physical volume buttons on the left side of your iPhone. These are the same buttons that you use to adjust the ringer volume and call volume, too. So, those are the basics for playing, pausing, fast-forwarding, rewinding, and controlling your volume.

Your Options When Playing a Song

When you're playing a song, some controls appear at the very top of the screen. To return to the previous screen, tap the Back button at the top left (for example, if you were listening to a playlist, it takes you back to the Playlists screen). If you tap the button at the top right, it takes you to a list of songs from that album (if you have more than one song from that album, you'll see them all listed there. If this is the only song you have from this album, it'll only list this one song). This is also where you can rate the current song (using a 1- to 5-star rating system. See page 208 for more on ratings). If you tap the center of the screen, another set of controls appears near the top of the screen, with four different options: (1) tap the button on the bottom left to repeat the song or playlist, (2) use the slider in the top center to "scrub" (move) through the song, (3) tap the button on the bottom right to shuffle the songs in that album or playlist, and (4) tap the atom icon at the bottom center to have the Music app create a Genius playlist of similar songs based on the song that's playing (see page 212 for more on Genius playlists).

---

iTip: Control Your Music from Your Lock Screen

If your iPhone is locked, you can still control your music without unlocking it—just double-tap the Home button and your Music app controls appear at the top of the screen.

Shuffle Your Songs

By default, your Music app plays the songs in the order they appear in your playlists, but that can get really repetitive after a while, and it doesn't take long before you pretty much know which song is coming next. That's why the Shuffle (random) feature is so popular. Just go to the very top of any playlist, and tap on **Shuffle** (shown above), and now your Music app will pick and play songs in a random order. Also, if you're listening to a playlist without Shuffle turned on and decide you want to turn it on, you don't have to go digging through any screens, all you have to do is physically shake your iPhone back and forth, and Shuffle kicks in (it sounds weird until you try it, but it's actually kind of a fun, organic way to turn on a feature).

---

iTip: Shuffling When Your Phone Is Locked

If your iPhone has gone to sleep while you're listening to your Music app, and you shake it, it won't shuffle because the phone is locked. But, there's a trick to get around that—just double-click on the Home button and the Music app controls appear (even though your phone is locked), and once you see those, you can shake to turn on the Shuffle feature.

Scrubbing Through a Song

The term "scrubbing" comes from the world of video editing, and it basically means that once a video is playing, you can grab the progress bar's slider knob and quickly move (scrub) it forward or backward through a video's timeline, seeing the video in fast speed as you move in either direction. The iPhone has this too, but your iPhone's scrubbing isn't just for video—you can scrub forward/backward through a song, podcast, audiobook, music video, etc., and you can not only go fast, but can also go very slowly and precisely if you want. You do this using the **progress bar** that appears onscreen (shown above circled in red) when a song or video is playing (if you don't see it, tap once on the screen and it will appear). If you tap-and-hold on the knob and drag left or right, you're in High-Speed Scrubbing mode (and it will say "Hi-Speed Scrubbing" right above the bar itself), but if you tap-and-hold on the knob and slide your finger downward, you'll see it change to Half Speed, Quarter Speed, and then Fine Scrubbing for very small movements.

Repeating a Song or Playlist

Start playing the song that you want to repeat or a song from the playlist that you want to repeat. Tap on the album art and you'll notice a little **circular arrows button** at the bottom left of the progress bar (circled above in red). This allows you to turn on Repeat. There are two modes to Repeat: Tapping the Repeat button once will repeat the entire playlist after all the songs have been played. Tapping the Repeat button again will show the circular arrow Repeat button with a 1 on it. This means that the current song will repeat over and over until you stop it. Tap the Repeat button one more time to turn Repeat off.

---

iTip: Playing Songs by Artist

*If you're in the mood to hear some Heart but you didn't create a specific Heart playlist, just tap the Artists button at the bottom of the screen for a list of all your artists then tap Heart. You'll see a choice between All Songs and their individual albums (if you only have one album for that artist, then you'll just see the songs). You'll see a list of albums even if you don't have all the songs on any of the given albums. You can tap **All Songs** to see a list of all the songs you have by that artist and then tap on a song to play them or you can tap a specific album to just play the songs on that album.*

Using Cover Flow

Cover Flow gives you a very cool, visual way of browsing through your music collection by seeing the album covers. To use Cover Flow, tap on the Music app. Once you're in the Music app, simply hold up your iPhone and turn it sideways in either direction. This will automatically switch the display to Cover Flow, and you now see your album cover art (or the music symbol, if a particular song doesn't have cover art). You can flick your finger across the screen to move through your albums. Once you find an album that you're interested in, tap on it and it will flip over to reveal the songs on that album. You can tap any song in that list to play it, and it will continue playing that album until it runs out of songs. To pause, press the tiny Pause button in the bottom-left corner of Cover Flow. To return to Cover Flow, tap the name of the album at the top, and the album flips back over and you're back looking at your album covers.

---

iTip: Another Way to Flip Albums

*You can also flip albums over and back by tapping the little **"i" button** in the lower-right corner of the Cover Flow screen.*

Rating Your Songs on the iPhone

While it's great that you can rate your songs as 1- to 5-star on your computer in iTunes, sometimes it's more convenient to rate songs right on your iPhone itself. To rate the currently playing song, tap the Track List button in the upper-right corner of the album art. The album art will flip over and you will see either **five dots** or the current rating that the song has. You can then tap the appropriate star/dot to rate your song as 1- to 5-star. Once you're done rating it, just tap the little Album Art button in the upper-right corner to return to your album art display. The next time you sync your iPhone to your computer, the ratings you made on your iPhone will be applied to those songs in iTunes on your computer (if you have this preference set).

---

iTip: Playing Other Songs from the Same Album

To access songs from the same album as the song that is currently playing, start any song playing in the Music app that has at least two songs from the same album. Now tap the little Track List button in the top-right corner of the screen (to the right of the song's name). This will flip the album over and reveal the other songs that you have on that album. You can start playing any song you want on that list without having to go find it elsewhere.

Sing Along with the Lyrics

If you've taken the time to find the lyrics to your favorite songs, you can paste them into the Lyrics section for that particular song in iTunes on your computer (by clicking on the song in your Music Library, choosing **Get Info** from the File menu, and then clicking on the Lyrics tab). The next time you sync your iPhone, the updated song will be downloaded to it with the lyrics (if you have this preference set). To display the lyrics of a song that is playing on your iPhone, simply tap the album art that is currently displaying. To hide the lyrics again, just tap the lyrics, and they will go away and the album art will be displayed again.

Using Your Playlists

Playlists are groups of songs you create (like a collection of your favorite songs by big hair bands of the '80s, or music you've put together for a road trip, or your favorite alternative songs, and so on). You can create these playlists on your computer in iTunes (or right on your iPhone; see the next page), and then you choose which playlists get synced to your iPhone from iTunes (when you have your iPhone plugged into your computer, click on it in the Devices list on the left side of the iTunes window, then click the Music tab in the center. This is where you choose which playlists get copied over). To play the songs in one of these playlists, tap on the Music app, then tap on the **Playlists button** at the bottom of the screen to see your list of playlists. Tap on a playlist and it shows you the list of songs in that playlist. Tap on any song, and it will play the songs in just this one playlist in order.

📶 iTip: You Can Have Loads of Playlists Without Taking Up Space

The great thing about playlists is that you can have as many as you want without it eating up all of your iPhone's memory, because the same song(s) can be in multiple playlists without taking up additional space. For example, let's say you have a playlist called "Male Vocals," one called "Quiet Storm," and one called "My Favorite T-Pain Songs." All three playlists could contain T-Pain's "5 O'Clock" track, but that song will only be copied to your iPhone once, no matter how many playlists it's in. So, create as many playlists as you like—it won't affect your storage space.

Creating New Playlists

Your iPhone also has a Music app feature that lets you create regular playlists right within the Music app itself. Here's how it's done: Start by first tapping on the Playlists button at the bottom of the Music app screen, then tap **Add Playlist** and a screen will appear asking you to name your new playlist. Type in a name, and tap Save. Once you tap it, you'll see a list of all your songs. Tap on the songs you want to add to your new playlist, and as you tap a song, the song's title turns gray to let you know it has been added. When you're done adding songs, tap the Done button in the upper-right corner and it displays the songs in your new playlist. If you want to edit this playlist, just tap the Edit button in the top-left corner, and now you can delete a song by tapping the red – (minus sign) button to the left of the song's title, then tapping the red Delete button that appears to the right (if you change your mind, just tap the red – button again). To change the order of the songs, tap-and-drag the triple-line icon to the right of the song you want to move. You can add more songs by tapping the + (plus sign) button in the top-left corner of the screen. When you're done editing, tap the Done button at the top of the screen. If you want to start over, tap the Clear button at the top of the screen, then tap Clear Playlist, and it removes all the songs from the playlist. If you want to get rid if it, just tap the Delete button, then tap Delete Playlist. Now this new playlist is added to your regular list of playlists, and you can create as many of these as you like.

Creating Genius Playlists on Your iPhone

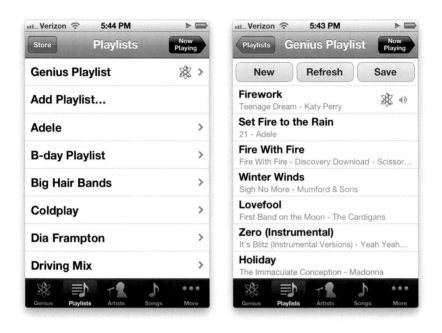

If you're working out and this really great track comes on that gets you totally pumped, and you think to yourself, "I wish I had a playlist of more stuff like this," well, your Music app can automatically search through your songs and create a playlist based on that track you're listening to. You just tap on the **atom-looking icon** that appears onscreen when you tap on the album art of the song playing. Of course, you don't have to have a song playing to make a Genius playlist: just tap on the Playlists button at the bottom of the screen, then tap on **Genius Playlist** up at the top of the list, and it will bring up the list of songs in your Music app. For example, if I tapped on "Bad Medicine" by Bon Jovi (hey, I like Bon Jovi) in my (Scott's) Music app, it would make a 25-song playlist and include songs like "Shake Me" by Cinderella, "Let It Go" by Def Leppard, "Little Suzi" by Tesla, "18 and Life" by Skid Row, and so on. By the way, once it has created a Genius playlist for you, it starts playing it right away, but if you tap the Back arrow at the top left of the screen, it'll not only display the songs in the Genius playlist, but it'll give you three buttons across the top: tap New to create a totally new Genius playlist; tap Refresh if you don't like the playlist it created and you want it to try again; or if you love that playlist and want to save it, tap Save. (*Note:* In order to use this feature, you must have the Genius feature turned on in iTunes on your computer. Once you sync your iPhone to your computer with the Genius feature enabled, you'll be able to create Genius playlists directly on your iPhone.)

Sharing Your Favorite Podcasts

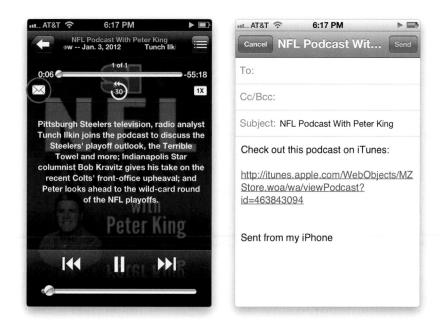

Once you've downloaded some audio podcasts (in the iTunes app, tap on More at the bottom, then tap on Podcasts), if you come across one that you really like, you can send a direct link to that podcast to a friend. Tap on the Music app, tap on More at the bottom of the screen, then tap on Podcasts. Here you'll see the audio podcasts that you down-loaded. Tap on one that you want to share, then while it's playing, tap on the **envelope icon** that appears near the upper-left corner of the screen (if you don't see these controls, just tap in the middle of the screen). When you tap on that icon, it launches Mail, creates a new email message, and inserts the direct link to that podcast in the iTunes Store (which is where you go to download free podcasts). It even enters the podcast's name in the Subject field, and tells the recipient to "Check out this podcast on iTunes." All you have to do is enter your friend's email address and tap Send.

Listening to Audiobooks

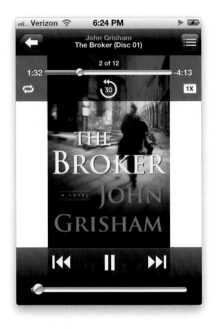

The iTunes Store has loads of audiobooks you can download, and you can buy them either on your computer or right on your iPhone itself. Unlike songs, the iPhone remembers right where you left off with an audiobook, whether you started listening to it in iTunes or on your iPhone, so you can listen in either place and the next time you sync to your computer, iTunes will update the audiobook to remember exactly where you left off (if you have this preference set). To listen to an audiobook on your iPhone, tap the More button at the bottom of the Music app screen, then tap **Audiobooks**. Now tap the audiobook you want to listen to. The Next/Fast Forward and Previous/Rewind buttons will advance you to the next chapter or take you back to the previous one. Also, you can change the speed of your audiobooks using the Playback Speed button near the top right of the screen (tap on the book's cover if you don't see this control). More than likely, you'll use this to speed the audiobook up to double-speed (I wish they had a 1.5x speed), but you can also slow it down by tapping on it.

---

iTip: Jump Back 30 Seconds for Audiobooks and Podcasts

If you're listening to an audiobook or audio podcast, or watching a video podcast, near the top of the screen you'll see a circular arrow with a 30 in the center of it. If you tap on it, it jumps back 30 seconds. This is great if you need to take a note, or write down a Web address that was mentioned and went by too quickly.

Taking a Call While You're Listening to Music

SCOTT KELBY

If you receive a call while you're using the Music app, the sound will automatically fade and you'll hear your phone ring. The iPhone will give you the choice of answering the call or declining it (which will send the caller to voicemail). If you answer the call, then you'll be taken to the iPhone's call screen. Once you end the call, the iPhone will pick up right where it left off playing your song, video, audiobook, etc. If you're listening to music (or audiobooks, video, etc.) with the Apple headset that came with your iPhone, you can press the tiny **microphone button** on the right earbud cable once to pause what's playing. To start playing it again, just press the button again.

Using the Audio Playback Control Widget

There's a built-in widget for quickly playing, pausing, rewinding, fast-forwarding, or controlling the volume of the music playing in your Music app, or audio streaming from the iTunes app (like an audio podcast or other audio app [like Pandora]). To get to this handy little widget anytime (no matter where you are in your iPhone), double-click the **Home button**, and the multitasking bar appears at the bottom of the screen. Now swipe to the right, and the control widget appears (seen above). Swipe to the right once more, and you'll see a volume slider. To control your music, tap the Play/Pause button, etc., then tap back anywhere on your screen area (basically, tap anywhere above the widget) to return to what you were doing, and your music continues to play in the background.

---

iTip: Locking Your Screen Orientation

*That little control widget has an extra feature—if you tap the **circular arrow button** on the far left side, it locks your screen in portrait (tall) orientation, so if you turn your screen sideways, it doesn't flip to a wide view like it normally would.*

Using External Speakers or Headsets

The dock connector on the bottom of your iPhone is similar to the dock connector on the bottom of a regular iPod, so you can usually connect your iPhone to an external speaker system made for an iPod (like the JBL On Stage shown above). However, since the iPhone is a GSM-based phone, its built-in radio could interfere with your stereo or speakers. In fact, when you plug your iPhone into a speaker system built for the iPod (not for the iPhone), you might get a message that says, "This accessory is not made to work with iPhone. Would you like to turn on Airplane Mode to reduce audio interference (you will not be able to make or receive calls)?" Turning on Airplane mode turns off the phone and Bluetooth portions of the iPhone, so it doesn't interfere with your stereo speakers. The only downside to this is that when your iPhone is in Airplane mode, you won't be able to make or receive calls. That's why we recommend trying it with your speakers first, without going into Airplane mode, and if there's no interference, you're home free. Another way around this problem is to use Apple's iPhone Dock (available at the Apple Store), which has a stereo line out port that can be used to connect directly to your stereo system. You can also connect wirelessly through AirPlay to some speakers, as mentioned earlier. Your iPhone also has a stereo headphone jack on the top, and if you want to use your own headphones you can, but there may be an issue actually plugging them in. The iPhone's headset jack is recessed and because of that some headset plugs may not be skinny enough to fit down in there. Luckily, Belkin, Monster, and Griffin Technologies have made adapters you can order online.

Setting a Sleep Timer

A sleep timer will play your music until the timer expires and then it will put the iPhone to sleep. To set a sleep timer, first go to your Music app and start playing the songs you want to play until the timer goes off. You can use a playlist (such as your "sleepy land" playlist—I know you have one—or any other playlist on your iPhone). Then press the Home button to go to the Home screen. Now tap Clock and then tap Timer. You can set the minutes, or hours and minutes, that you want the music to play before going to sleep. Next, tap the When Timer Ends button and choose **Sleep iPod**. Then tap the Set button in the upper-right corner of the screen to return to the Timer screen. Now tap Start to begin the countdown. When the timer reaches the end of its set time, the music will fade and the iPhone will go to sleep.

Rearranging Your Music Buttons

When you go to the Music app, you'll see buttons at the bottom of the screen for Genius, Playlists, Artists, Songs, and More. When you tap the More button, you'll see that you have a lot more options (Albums, Audiobooks, Compilations, Composers, Genres, iTunes U, and Podcasts). However, if you use any of these more often than the default buttons on the main Music screen, you can swap them. To move a button from the More screen to the main Music screen, tap the **Edit button** in the upper-left corner of the More screen. You'll then see buttons for all the Music app categories. Simply drag the button you want to move over the top of the button at the bottom that you want to replace with it, and when the existing button highlights, you can let go. When you've got the buttons you want in the order you want them, tap Done.

iTip: Moving Your Primary Music App Buttons

While you're choosing which buttons you want to be your primary Music app buttons, you can also drag the ones that are there in a different order. For example, on my iPhone they are now listed as Playlists, Artists, Podcasts, Genius and More. In the Configure screen, simply drag them in the order you want them listed.

Chapter Twelve

Video Killed the Radio Star

Using the Videos App

 It's hard to believe, but the 1979 song "Video Killed the Radio Star," from The Buggles, actually has an important place in music history because when MTV went live back in August 1981, their debut music video was (you guessed it) "Video Killed the Radio Star." I have a regular iPod that does play video, but it doesn't have the larger, more luxurious widescreen display the iPhone has, and it was while pondering that thought, I realized the iPhone itself was playing a role in music history, and as an iPhone owner, like MTV, I would have to choose which music video would debut on my iPhone. Knowing that my choice would, in some small way, be part of my own personal music history really put a lot of pressure on me. I mean, think about it—years from now, it's quite possible that sociology students at colleges in far off places, like Helsinki (or Cleveland), might one day study, debate, and pick apart my music video debut choice, and I'm not sure I can deal with that kind of responsibility. And that's probably why, when I was carefully scrolling through my music video collection, rather than "flicking" or "swiping," I accidentally tapped the Play button right when the Spice Girls' "Wannabe" video was scrolling by, and I swear it felt like I went into some kind of slow motion dream state as I scrambled and fumbled to tap the Pause button…but it was too late. There it was, playing full screen. My only solace was, like The Buggles, the Spice Girls are British. If you listen carefully, you can almost hear the university professors in Helsinki giggling as they type their fall course descriptions.

Launching the Videos App

In iOS 5, Apple split up the old iPod app into two different apps: Music and Videos. The Videos app can be launched from your Home screen (I put all my video-related apps into a folder on my Home screen) and, from there, you can play back any movies, TV shows, video podcasts, and music videos that you have loaded on your iPhone.

Watching Videos on Your iPhone

You can watch movies, TV shows, music videos, and video podcasts on your iPhone that you download from iTunes or the iTunes Store. To watch a video, just tap on it in the video list, and it will start playing. You can access the controls while it's playing by just tapping the screen. There are two screen modes: full screen and widescreen. To toggle between them, double-tap the screen. In widescreen mode, you'll see the entire video from edge to edge. If the video is at a different aspect ratio, then it may have black bars at the top and bottom or left and right. You can also play it full screen, so that there are no bars, but some of the video may be cropped off. *Note:* If you shot video with your iPhone's built-in camera, those videos don't appear in the Videos app—they're in the Photos app, in your Camera Roll.

---

iTip: Watching Your Own Home Movies

You can convert your home movies in QuickTime format into the proper format right in iTunes (if it's not in the QuickTime format, see the iTip on the next page). Add the movie to your iTunes Library and choose **Create iPod or iPhone Version** *from the Advanced menu.*

Watching Videos Not Yet on Your iPhone

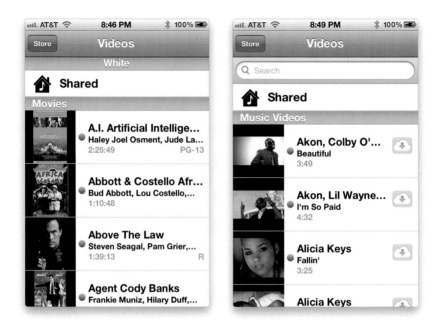

It's great that you can watch videos on your iPhone that you've synced from iTunes on your computer, or ones that you've downloaded from the iTunes Store, but you can also watch videos that are in iTunes on your computer or music videos in iCloud *before* you actually put them on your iPhone. With Home Sharing enabled both in your Settings app's Videos app settings and in your iTunes Preferences, you'll be able to access *all* of your iPhone-compatible videos via your Wi-Fi network. Just tap on **Shared** at the top of the Videos list and then choose any of the iTunes libraries running on your network that is logged into the same Home Sharing account. If you have an iTunes Match account and you have some music videos in iCloud, you'll be able to play/download those whenever you have an Internet connection, even if you're not at home. They will appear in your Videos list under Music Videos, with a cloud icon next to any of the ones that you haven't downloaded yet.

---

iTip: Watching Purchased DVDs

iTunes doesn't convert regular movie DVDs that you purchased, like it does with CDs, but there is a workaround. Before I go any further, you'll have to check the laws in your country and the license agreements of the DVDs you've purchased to make sure that you aren't breaking any laws by converting them for your own personal use on another device, such as the iPhone. To convert a purchased movie DVD, you're going to need an additional program. My favorite one is called Handbrake. It's cross-platform and, best of all, it's free! Remember, this process is for your own personal use only.

Getting Movies, Music Videos, and TV Shows from iTunes

You can get video content from the iTunes app directly on your iPhone without having to go to your computer first. Just tap the **Store button** in the upper-left corner of the Videos app (or tap on **iTunes** on your Home screen). You can buy or rent movies and you can buy music videos and TV shows. You'll need a Wi-Fi connection to download the videos from the iTunes Store. If you buy something, you'll be able to keep it and watch it as many times as you want. The video will also be synced back to your computer the next time you sync your iPhone with iTunes. Movies that you rent will be available to start watching for up to 30 days. Once you start watching, you'll have 24 hours to finish watching it or to watch it as many times as you want within that time. Then, it will automatically delete itself.

---

iTip: What Happens When You Lose Wi-Fi During a Download?

If you're downloading a video larger than 20 MB (so, just about any movie applies), you have to be on a Wi-Fi network to start your downloading process, but if you move out of range of your Wi-Fi connection, your iPhone will continue the download using its cellular network. Of course, it will take a lot longer, but at least it'll work.

Movie DVDs That Contain a Digital Copy

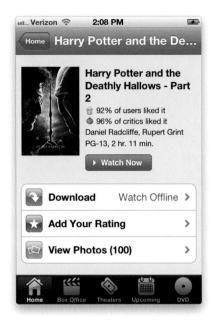

Some movie studios selling Blu-ray discs and DVDs include a digital copy (on a second disc) that is already formatted for your iPhone. It's the best of both worlds. You get a DVD or Blu-ray disc to watch on your big-screen TV, and you get a second disc that you put into your computer. Once you authorize the digital copy to your iTunes account, it's automatically copied into iTunes and is available to sync to your iPhone. The next time you're buying a movie on DVD or Blu-ray, be sure to check the packaging to see if it includes a digital copy. Some movie studios are including redemption codes for a digital download, instead, although these may require you to download a third-party app, such as Flixster (seen above), to watch the movie on your iPhone.

---

iTip: What Happens When You Buy an HD Movie on Your iPhone

*If you buy an HD movie on your iPhone, what gets downloaded to your iPhone isn't an HD movie, it's the standard definition version that is designed to work perfectly with your iPhone (which isn't HD), but when you get back to your computer, the HD version will be waiting to be downloaded from iTunes at no extra charge. Once you sign in, it should start downloading to your Movies Library. If not, just click on **Downloads** in the Source list on the left side of the iTunes window, and click the down arrow button at the bottom.*

TiVo To Go

If you own a TiVo Series 2, Series 3, or TiVo HD, then you can transfer most of your recorded TV shows or movies from your TiVo to your computer using TiVo's TiVo-To-Go option. On a PC, there is a TiVo-To-Go app that you can download directly from TiVo's website (TiVo Desktop Plus software for PC). On a Mac, this functionality is available through Roxio's Toast Titanium software CD/DVD burning app. Once you have the TiVo-To-Go option set up, you can transfer unrestricted TV shows or movies directly from your TiVo DVR to your Mac or PC over your home network. Then, you can use the TiVo or Toast software to convert it to a format that will play on your iPhone. Depending on the size of the show (standard definition vs. HD), it could take several minutes or hours to transfer the content and convert it, so plan ahead.

iTip: Set Your TiVo with Your iPhone

If you are a TiVo user, you can access most of the great features of the main TiVo website by going to their iPhone-friendly website using your iPhone's Safari app. Just go to m.tivo .com. Once you log in, it even remembers your password for you. It's a great way to schedule recordings while you're on the go! TiVo also has its own app that lets you control your DVR with your iPhone without interrupting the currently playing show.

Connect Your iPhone to Your TV

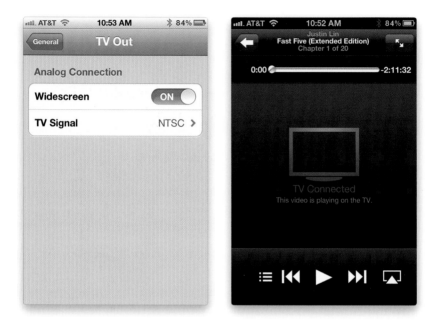

All you need is either the Apple Component AV Cable or the Apple Composite AV Cable, and you can enjoy your movies, TV shows, podcasts, and music videos on the big screen. The Apple Composite AV cable is for connecting to TVs (or projectors) with standard RCA-style connectors—yellow for video, and red and white for stereo audio. However, if you have a newer TV (or HD projector), chances are it has component jacks on the back, which would be red, green, and blue, as well as red and white stereo inputs. So, make sure you check out your TV to see which connections it has before buying your cable. Also, included with these cables is an additional AC-to-USB adapter, so you'll have power to your iPhone while it's playing. This way, you can just leave the cable connected to your TV at all times if you like. Once you have the cable connected to your TV and iPhone, go to the Settings app and tap General, then tap **TV Out** (you won't see TV Out until the cable is connected). You can have the iPhone display the appropriate format by turning Widescreen on, if you have a 16:9 widescreen TV, and choose between NTSC or PAL, depending upon the standard supported in your country. Once you've chosen the appropriate settings, tap the Home button, and then tap the Videos app. Then, find the video you want to watch, and make sure your TV is on the appropriate input for either your composite or component connection. You should then be able to start your video and see it on the big screen. Also, while your movie or video is playing, your iPhone serves as a remote that lets you pause, skip chapters, etc.

Using AirPlay to Stream Video to Your Apple TV

If you have an Apple TV 2 or newer, you can actually stream video content wirelessly through your Apple TV so that you can enjoy it on the big screen. You have be on the same Wi-Fi network as your Apple TV. Then, just start your video playing and tap the little **AirPlay button** on the onscreen controls. You'll get a list of AirPlay-compatible devices, including your Apple TV, and once you choose it, the video will be playing on your TV instead of your iPhone. It's probably best to plug your iPhone into a power source if you're watching a long movie.

iTip: Deleting Videos on Your iPhone

*You can delete videos directly from the iPhone to make more room. On the Video or episode screen, flick your finger across the title of the video to get a red **Delete button**. Tap it and the video is deleted from your iPhone immediately.*

Chapter Thirteen

One Hour Photo

Using Your Camera and Working with Photos and Videos

 I chose the movie *One Hour Photo* as this chapter's title after realizing that my song title choices were pretty much either "Photos of Toast" by Ectogram or "Photos of Nothing" by Southeast Engine. I was leaning towards "Photos of Toast" until I heard "Photos of Nothing," and I knew right then I needed to find something more productive to do for a living other than searching the iTunes Store for songs that contain the word "photo." But I digress. I could have gone with two more obvious choices like "Photograph" from Ringo Starr or Def Leppard. Personally, I like Def Leppard's "Photograph," because I feel cooler lip syncing to them whilst holding a pool cue than I do when singing Ringo's song, which you want to avoid doing in any bar that has a pool table. Luckily that's not a big fear of mine because the odds of finding a jukebox with Ringo's "Photograph" on it (the one that starts with "Every time I see your face, it reminds me of the places we used to go. But all I've got is a photograph…") are less than winning the Powerball lottery. That's because Ringo just isn't very big with the pool hall crowd, which is, by the way, a crowd that does favor Def Leppard for one simple reason: Def Leppard is in the Pool Cue Air Guitar Hall of Fame. Sadly, it wasn't for "Photograph"—it was for "Pour Some Sugar On Me," which would have made a great chapter name if the iPhone had either Pouring or Sugar Dispensing features. Sadly, it has neither. I know what you're thinking, "He should have gone with 'Photos of Toast.'" That's not what you were thinking, was it?

Using the Built-In Camera

SCOTT KELBY

To get to the camera, just tap the Camera app (shown circled above) and you'll see a full-color image of what you're pointing your iPhone at (the camera is on the back side of the iPhone—on the top left). A white square will appear briefly to show you what you're focusing on (more about this on page 238). To take a picture, tap the pill-shaped button with a camera icon on it (the shutter button) at the bottom of the screen. You'll hear a shutter sound (like a regular camera), and then you'll see a graphic like a shutter opening and closing, so you know that it took the photo. If you have an iPhone 4S, you can actually use the Volume Up button on the side of your iPhone as your shutter button, as well. Once you take a photo, it's added to your Camera Roll (where all your photos are stored), and your camera is ready to take the next photo. If you want to quickly see the photo you just took, swipe to the right on the screen. To return to the camera, swipe to the left. To see the photos in your Camera Roll, tap the little square in the bottom-left corner of the screen.

---

iTip: Shooting Wide Photos

If you want to shoot your photos in landscape (wide) orientation, just turn your iPhone sideways. To shoot in portrait (tall) orientation, just keep it turned upright.

The Second Camera in Your iPhone

If you have an iPhone 4 or 4S, you have a second camera—one on the front of your iPhone, so you can make FaceTime (video) calls. However, this second camera is great for taking self-portraits (or a portrait of you and a friend). To turn on this second camera, just tap the **Camera Swap button** (the camera with circular arrows) in the top-right corner of the screen. When you do this, it shows you the view from the camera on the front of your iPhone. Just hold it out if front of you (you'll see a live preview onscreen) and then just tap the shutter button (the pill-shaped button at the bottom center of the screen with a camera icon on it) to take a photo of yourself. To switch back to the regular camera, tap the Camera Swap button again.

---

iTip: Seeing an Onscreen "Rules of Thirds" Grid

To see a visible grid over your image (to help you compose your image using the photog-raphy "Rule of Thirds"), in the Camera app, tap on the Options button at the top of the screen, then tap on the **Grid Off button** to turn it on, and then tap the Done button. This grid visually divides the scene into horizontal and vertical thirds—handy when you're trying to make sure your camera is straight when you're taking a landscape shot or a shot with a horizon line.

Taking HDR (High Dynamic Range) Photos

Your iPhone camera has a built-in HDR feature that works wonderfully well in tricky lighting situations (like when part of the photo is really bright and part is really dark, which usually wreaks havoc on photos). When you turn this on (in the Camera app, tap on the Options button at the top center, then tap the **HDR Off button** to turn it on), your camera automatically captures a wider range of exposure, which balances the light in the photo so it captures more detail. By default, when you take a photo with the HDR feature turned on, you take two photos: (1) the original photo, and (2) the HDR photo. Since they're right next to each other, you can swipe back and forth between them and keep the one that looks the best (you can delete the one you don't like by just tapping once on the Trash button at the bottom of the screen).

---

iTip: My Favorite HDR App

If you're really into HDR photography, try my favorite HDR app, True HDR (available in the App Store for 99¢). I like to use its manual mode, where you first tap on the brightest thing in the image, then take a photo. Then, you tap on the darkest thing in the photo and take that photo. Then you tap the Merge button, and it aligns and combines the two images (one dark, one bright) into a single image with the best of both photos combined. I love it (and hope you will, too)!

Editing Your Photos Right on Your iPhone

In iOS 5, you can do some key photo editing tasks right on your iPhone—things like cropping, rotating, removing red eye, and even enhancing the overall exposure of your photo. Start by tapping on the photo you want edit in your Camera Roll (or other album), then tap the **Edit button** at the top-right corner of the screen. This brings up a menu bar along the bottom of the screen. To rotate your image, tap the Rotate button (on the left). To automatically enhance the overall look of the photo, tap the Auto Enhance button (right next to the Rotate button; it looks like a magic wand). Auto Enhance does a pretty amazing job in most cases, giving you more vibrant, colorful, and contrasty photos. The next button to the right (the round red circle with a line through it) is the Remove Red-Eye button. If you have a photo where somebody has the dreaded red-eye reflection in their eyes, tap this button, then tap right on each eye to "get the red out." The last editing tool (on the right) is the Crop button. To crop your image, tap on this button, then tap-and-drag your finger inward on any of the corners of the cropping border. If you want the photo to be a specific size, once you've resized the border, tap the Constrain button and choose a size. Then, you can reposition the photo within the border by just dragging it around with your finger.

Arranging Your Photos in Albums

SCOTT KELBY

Once you've taken a bunch of photos, you might want to arrange them into photo albums (like a Family album, or a Vacation album, and so on), so you can see groups of related images quickly with just one tap. To create an album, tap on the Photos app, and then tap the Edit button in the top-right corner of the Albums screen. Next, tap the **Add button** in the upper-left corner, give your new album a name, and tap Save. Now your Camera Roll, Photo Library, Photo Stream (if you have it turned on; more about this on page 260), and a list of any other albums you've created will appear for you to find the photos you want to add to your new album. Tap on whichever album the photos are in, then tap on Select All Photos or tap each photo you want added (a blue circle with a checkmark will appear on each photo's thumbnail to let you know it has been selected). Once you've got all the photos you want selected, just tap the blue Done button (at the top right) and those photos will be added to your new album. To see it, just tap on it in your Albums list. To delete a photo from an album, just tap on it, then tap the Trash button at the bottom of the screen. Don't worry, this only removes the photo from that album, it doesn't delete it from your iPhone.

Your Camera Can Get Really, Really Close

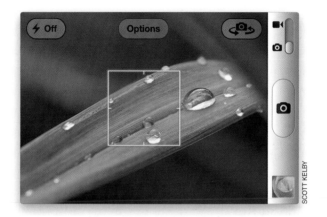

Your iPhone's camera has an automatic macro feature for taking really close-up photos. In fact, it will focus up to just a few inches from the object you're trying to shoot (you can get as close as 4" away, and it will still focus). You may be thinking, "Why would I want a photo taken that close to anything?" Actually, it's fun (it's one of those things you just have to try for yourself). In fact, go ahead and try it right now—grab your iPhone, tap the Camera app, get around 4"–5" from something, and you'll see that the macro auto-focus kicks right in. I know. It's cooler than it sounds.

iTip: The Shortcut for Getting to the Camera Fast

If your iPhone is locked, there's a shortcut to get you to the Camera app really fast— so fast, you don't even have to unlock it (that way you don't miss the shot while you're fumbling around to unlock it): just double-click the Home button and a Camera button appears to the right of your Slide to Unlock button on the Lock screen. Tap it and you're ready to shoot! (Well, take a photo. You knew what I meant, right?)

How to Choose Where to Focus

SCOTT KELBY

Another great feature of the camera in the iPhone is its ability to focus right where you want it—you just tap on the thing you want it to focus on. That way, you can choose whether you want the camera to focus on something near you, or something farther away. When you're focusing, a little white square will appear onscreen that shows you what the camera is currently focusing on. If you want to change the focus to something else, just tap on that other thing. By the way, this "tap on what you want in focus" thing isn't just for focus. Where you tap is also the area the camera then uses to set the overall exposure for the photo and white balance, and this helps you get better-looking photos overall. One more thing: if something in your photo will be moving (like maybe a toddler, or your pet), then tap-and-hold for a moment. That locks the focus, so if they move, the focus doesn't jump over onto something else.

---

iTip: Shooting Over Your Head

Although we say "tap" the shutter button, sometimes it's better to press-and-hold the button until the moment you're ready to shoot. For example, if you're holding your iPhone up high (maybe over a crowd), it'll be hard to see right where to tap, so you might miss the shot. Instead, press-and-hold the shutter button while the camera is still right in front of you, and keep your finger held down on it as you raise up the camera. Then, to take the shot, you just remove your finger. This is also a great tip for taking self-portraits with the iPhone 3GS (since you can't see the screen).

Using the Built-In Zoom Feature

To zoom in on a particular area, just put your fingers together on the spot you want to zoom in on (like you're going to pinch something), then just spread them outward and it zooms in, and a **digital zoom slider** appears onscreen. Drag that slider to the right (toward the plus sign) to zoom in closer to your subject, and back to the left to zoom back out to normal. There is one thing you need to know about this zooming: it's digital zoom, rather than optical zoom, so the zooming is done in the software—the lens itself doesn't extend like a traditional camera lens. So, you lose a little picture quality when you zoom in digitally like this (this isn't just an iPhone thing—the same thing applies to regular HD video cameras that offer "digital zoom").

iTip: Going Straight from Your Camera to Twitter

*Once you've taken a photo, if you want to put it up on Twitter, just tap on the Camera Roll button (in the bottom-left corner of the camera screen), then tap on the photo you want to tweet, and then tap the Share button at the bottom of the screen (it's a square with an arrow coming out of it). Tap the **Tweet button**, and this brings up a text field where you can type your tweet, and when you tap Send, your photo will automatically be attached and uploaded to Twitter along with your text.*

Using the Built-In Flash

On the back of your iPhone 4 or 4S, there's a small LED flash, and you can turn it on by tapping the **Flash button** (the button with the lightning bolt icon) in the top-left corner of the camera screen. This brings up a list of three flash options: (1) Off turns the flash off (I know, I didn't really need to explain that one); (2) Auto automatically turns the flash on if the camera senses it needs more light to make a decent picture; and (3) On turns the flash on whether you need it not.

iTip: Using Your Flash as a Flashlight

Shortly after the iPhone 4 came out with built-in flash, developers started introducing apps that let you keep the bright LED flash turned on, so you can use it as a flashlight (great for finding your car keys at night). There are a number of different flashlight apps out there, but the one I use is called Light-O-Matic, which sells for 99¢ (Terry picked it as his #1 pick for flashlight apps on his www.bestappsite.com, so I downloaded it right away and I love it).

Shooting Video with Your iPhone

The iPhone takes surprisingly good HD-quality video, and it couldn't be easier to use. Tap on the Camera app, and on the bottom right of the screen is a button where you choose between the still camera (the default choice) and the video camera. To shoot video, tap the button and it switches to video. Aim the camera where you want it, and if you need to focus on a particular person or object, tap the screen on that focus point (see page 238 on focusing). When you're ready to start recording your video, tap the button with the red dot at the bottom of the screen. You'll hear a "ding," and the red dot starts blinking to let you know you're now recording. When you want to stop recording, tap the blinking red dot button and you'll hear two dings (and the red dot stops blinking). Once you're finished recording, to see your video, tap the small square thumbnail in the lower-left corner of the screen, then tap the Play button to see (and hear) your video. Also, just in case you were wondering, your video gets saved into your Camera Roll, right alongside your photos.

Shooting Video with Your iPhone Widescreen

When you're shooting video, you'll probably want to turn your iPhone sideways, so you're shooting widescreen (like your TV). If you hold it straight up, you'll end up with a tall, skinny video (which kind of looks weird). Turning your iPhone sideways and shooting your video widescreen will give you larger videos, which are easier to see on your iPhone (or your computer, or TV).

iTip: Seeing Which Thumbnails Are Video

When you look on your Camera Roll screen, it's easy to see which thumbnails are photos and which are video. The video clips have a small movie camera icon in the bottom-left corner of the thumbnail, and the length of the video clip, in minutes and seconds, is listed on the bottom right.

Editing Video on Your iPhone

SCOTT KELBY

If your video has some extra space at the beginning or end, you can trim it down to size right on your iPhone. In fact, you can pretty much just pick and choose which part of the video you want. Here's how: Find the video you want to edit in the Camera Roll (from the Home screen, tap on Photos), or if you want to edit the video you just shot, then tap the little square thumbnail in the bottom-left corner of the screen when you're done shooting. This brings up your video clip. Tap the screen and a **Frame Viewer bar** appears at the top of the screen. You can drag your finger along this Frame Viewer to move to a particular part of the video clip. To trim your video to just the part you want, drag the left side of the Frame Viewer bar to where you want the video to start, then drag the right side of the Frame Viewer bar to where you want it to end. When you do this, the bar turns yellow, letting you know you're in Trim mode. Tap the Play button at the bottom of the screen to see your edited video clip. If you like it, tap the yellow **Trim button** at the top right, and it lops off that extra stuff on both ends, and now your video is cut down to size (so to speak).

---

iTip: Deleting a Video

*If you want to completely delete a video, just tap on its thumbnail in the Camera Roll (so it appears full screen), then tap on the Trash icon in the lower-right corner. When the menu appears, tap the **Delete Video button**.*

Video Straight from Your iPhone to YouTube

You can take video you've shot and publish it directly on YouTube.com right from your iPhone. Here's what you do: Once you've shot the video, tap on the thumbnail to bring it up full screen, and trim it down to the size you want (if necessary), then tap the button in the bottom-left corner of the video screen, and a menu will appear. Tap on **Send to YouTube**, and your iPhone will compress the video and take you to the Publish Video screen (shown above), but before that screen appears, it's going to ask you to enter your YouTube.com username and password (you have to have a free YouTube.com account before YouTube will let you publish any videos there, so if you don't have an account, go to their website and sign up for one, or this is as far as you can go). Enter a title and description of your video, then add any tags (search terms), choose a category that matches your video, and choose whether you want it to be Public, Unlisted, or Private. Now you're ready to tap the Publish button at the top right of the screen and your iPhone will upload your video to your YouTube.com account. Once it's uploaded, a menu will appear telling you that your video has been published, with buttons for watching it right now on YouTube.com (from your iPhone), or sending a friend the link to the YouTube video, so they can watch it on their phone (or their computer). If you tap the Tell a Friend button, it copies-and-pastes the YouTube.com direct Web link to your video into a new email message, and it puts the video's name as the subject line.

Your iPhone Treats Videos Like Photos

Well, that's pretty much true. Except for the fact that you can trim your video and send it up to YouTube.com, all the things in this chapter that pertain to working with photos on your iPhone also apply to video. For example, you delete a video the same way you delete a photo (tap on the Trash icon). To see a photo or a video full screen, just tap on it. You can email a video just like you email a photo, and you can send a video in a text message just like you can send a photo, although you can't tweet it or use the editing tools on it. You can even geotag videos just like you do photos (see the next page). You can choose where to focus the video camera, just like you do the still camera, and yes—it sets the video camera's exposure like that, too. So, you can pretty much figure, if you can do it to a photo, you can probably do it to a video, too!

---

iTip: Turn On the Flash for Shooting Video in the Dark

*If you have an iPhone 4 or 4S, when you shoot video, your camera's flash turns into a continuous light, so you can have some light when you're shooting video in the dark. To turn on your video light, go to the Camera app, slide the switch over to video, then tap the **Flash button** (the button with the lightning bolt) and choose On to light your video as you shoot.*

Want to See Where You Took That Photo?

This is pretty amazing. If you have Location Services turned on in your iPhone (go to the Settings app, tap Location Services, and turn it on. Also, make sure Camera is turned on in the list below), then your camera will automatically embed the GPS coordinates of where you took your photos as you take them. Some apps can actually show you on Google Maps where you were when you took the photo. Geotagging also places your photos on a world map on your iPhone. Just go to the Photos app and tap on **Places**. Little red pins on the map represent the places where you've taken photos or videos (you can pinch-and-slide your fingers outward to zoom in on the map). Tap on one of the pins, and it tells you how many photos and videos were taken at that particular place and shows you a thumbnail of the first one (as shown above). Tap the blue arrow, and it shows you thumbnails of all the photos and videos you took there. Also, if you upload your photos to Flickr.com, in the Flickr account preferences, you can turn on geotagging. Once it's turned on, photos from your iPhone will automatically appear on the map for your Flickr account.

---

iTip: Stopping the Auto-Rotation

You know how when you turn your iPhone sideways, the screen automatically switches to a wide landscape view? Right, it's really handy, but what if you're looking at a photo, or showing somebody a photo, and you don't want it to automatically rotate? Just lightly press your finger on the screen, and now it won't auto-rotate, even if you turn it sideways.

Add Your iPhone's Geotag Info to Other Photos Using iPhoto

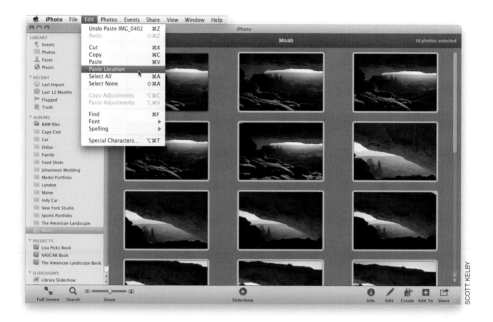

Each time you take a photo with your iPhone it captures location information, and you can use that information to geotag photos taken with your regular digital camera (if it doesn't have GPS). First, take a picture with your iPhone, then put it away and start shooting with your regular camera (be sure to shoot one photo with your iPhone each time you move to a different location). Import both your iPhone and your regular digital camera shots into iPhoto (which comes preinstalled on all new Macs). Select the first iPhone shot from the first location, Right-click on it, and choose Copy. Now select all the other photos from the same location, and from the Edit menu, choose **Paste Location**. iPhoto will then add the longitude and latitude location info to all the other photos. Just rinse-and-repeat for the rest of the shots from your shoot.

📶 iTip: Tag Your Photos with Faces

If you're a Mac user and you import your photos into iPhoto or Aperture, you can tag your photos with Faces and those groups of photos will appear when you tap the Faces button in the Photos app.

If You Shoot Video, Get iMovie for iPhone

Although you can do some simple video editing right on your iPhone (like trimming the length), you can't add background music, or titles, or combine multiple clips, or any of the other cool things you can do with Apple's iMovie app (just $4.99 from the App Store, but worth much more). This is an iPhone version of Apple's popular iMovie for the Mac, and it's really amazing what they've done with it—you can give your videos a slick, produced look, all from the palm of your hand. Here's how it works: Launch iMovie and tap the **Tap + to Start a New Project button** to start a new project. Choose one of their built-in themes (these pro-designed templates are what give your video that pro-quality look) and if you want, turn on Theme Music. Next, choose whether you want to use some video you've already shot or if you want to shoot something new (if you shoot something new, it'll automatically add a smooth fade between your video clips). Once your clips appear at the bottom of the screen, double-tap on any one of them to bring up the Clip Settings menu, where you can choose a Title Style for your theme (if you leave this set to None, you won't see the theme when you play your video), add some text, and make changes to your location and audio settings. To see a preview of your movie, tap the Play button. To see your full project, tap the star-on-a-page icon in the top left, and it takes you to a list of all your projects, and you can now see it full screen (by tapping the Play button at the bottom of the screen). Once you've completed your masterpiece, you can easily share it to your Camera Roll (for email and MMS), YouTube, Facebook, Vimeo, iTunes, and even CNN iReport (by tapping the icon with the arrow coming out of the box—you get to choose your final size at this point). Try it once, and you'll be a mini-moviemaker forever.

Getting Photos into Your iPhone (Mac)

If you're using a Mac, the easiest way to get photos into your iPhone is using Apple's iPhoto application (which comes pre-installed on all Macs). You drag-and-drop your photos right onto the iPhoto icon in your Mac's onscreen Dock and it imports them into your iPhoto Library. Then, click on the Create button near the bottom right to create separate photo albums (like one for family shots, or one for travel photos, one for your portfolio if you're a serious photographer, etc.), and drag-and-drop photos from the Library right onto the album of your choice. Once your photos are arranged in albums within iPhoto, when you connect your iPhone to your computer, it automatically uploads your photo albums to your iPhone (if you have this preference set). You can see your uploaded albums by going to the Photos app.

---

iTip: Uploading Specific Photo Albums

*You can set up your iPhone so only certain iPhoto albums are uploaded to it. You do this in iTunes when your iPhone is connected to your computer. On the left side of the iTunes window, under Devices, click on your iPhone to bring up its preferences. Click on the Photos tab, then turn on the Sync Photos From checkbox, and choose iPhoto from this pop-up menu. You'll see that the default setting has all of your iPhoto albums being uploaded. To choose just specific albums to be uploaded, click on the Selected Albums, Events, and Faces, and Automatically Include radio button, then turn on the checkboxes beside the albums, events, and faces you want uploaded. When you're done, click the **Apply button** in the bottom right.*

Getting Photos Without iPhoto (Mac)

If you don't want to use Apple's iPhoto application to manage the photos you want uploaded to your iPhone, you can just put them in a folder on your Mac and have iTunes do the uploading for you. Here's how: First, connect your iPhone to your computer, which brings up iTunes (if you have this preference set). In the Source list on the left side of the iTunes window, under Devices, click on your iPhone to bring up the iPhone preferences, then click on the Photos tab. At the top of this pane, turn on the Sync Photos From checkbox, and from this pop-up menu, select **Choose Folder**. This brings up a standard Open dialog, where you choose which folder your photos are in. Once you navigate your way to that folder, click the Open button, then go to the bottom-right corner of the iTunes window and click the **Apply button** to upload the photos in that folder to your iPhone. If you have photos in subfolders, they will show up as individual albums on your iPhone, and you can choose which of these subfolders are uploaded by clicking on the Selected Folders radio button near the top of the Photos pane, and turning on the checkboxes for only the subfolders you want on your iPhone. Easy enough.

---

iTip: Finding the Number of Photos in an Album

If you're looking inside an album on your iPhone, and want to know how many photos are in it without having to return to the main Albums screen, just scroll all the way to the bottom of the thumbnails and you'll see how many photos are in that album.

Getting Photos into Your iPhone (PC)

There is no version of Apple's iPhoto application for Windows, but your iPhone does support direct automatic importing from two other photo management applications: (1) Adobe Photoshop Album version 2 (which was a free application that Adobe offered, but has since discontinued). Or (2) any version of Adobe Photoshop Elements since version 3. To set this up, first connect your iPhone to your computer, which brings up iTunes. In the Source list on the left side of the iTunes window, under Devices, click on your iPhone to bring up the iPhone preferences, then click on the Photos tab. At the top of this pane, turn on the Sync Photos From checkbox, and from this pop-up menu, choose which one of the two supported applications you want to import from— Photoshop Album or Photoshop Elements. Now click the **Apply button** in the bottom-right corner to upload the photos to your iPhone.

---

iTip: Changing the Order of Your Photos

To change the order of your photos, you have to go back to your computer. Change the order the photos appear in the album, then go to iTunes, sync your iPhone with your computer, and it will update your iPhone with the new order.

Getting Photos Without Album or Elements (PC)

If you don't want to use Photoshop Album or Photoshop Elements to manage the photos you want uploaded to your iPhone, you can just put them in a folder on your PC and have iTunes do the uploading for you. Here's how: First, connect your iPhone to your computer, which brings up iTunes (if you have that preference set). In the Source list on the left side of the iTunes window, under Devices, click on your iPhone to bring up the iPhone prefer- ences, then click on the Photos tab. At the top of this pane, turn on the Sync Photos From checkbox, and from this pop-up menu, select **Choose Folder**. This brings up the Change Photos Folder Location dialog (it's like a standard Open dialog), where you choose which folder your photos are in. Once you've made your way to that folder, click the Select Folder button, then go to the bottom-right corner of the iTunes window, and click the **Apply button** to upload the photos in that folder to your iPhone. If you have subfolders in that folder, you can also click the Selected Folders radio button near the top of the Photos pane, and turn on the checkboxes only for the subfolders you want to upload. The subfolders will show up as albums on your iPhone.

iPhone Tips for Photographers

If you're a professional photographer or serious hobbyist, you've probably already figured out that the iPhone makes for a great tool to show off your shots. However, there are some other ways you can use the iPhone to help you with your future shoots. First of all, since the iPhone can have multiple albums, you can have multiple portfolios on hand to show friends, family, and prospective clients. You can also use the iPhone to display different lighting setups that you shot, as well as shots you'd like to do. You might also consider an album of various poses. This way, you can walk right over to your model and show them exactly how you'd like them to pose without them having to leave the set and walk over to your computer. The possibilities are endless. Just sync these albums from your computer to your iPhone the next time you connect them.

Viewing Your Imported Photos

Once you've imported photos into your iPhone, to see them, tap on the **Photos app**. This brings up the Albums screen and at the top is your Camera Roll (the photos taken with the iPhone's camera), then your Photo Library (all the photos you've imported into your iPhone all lumped together), and then a list of any separate photo albums you created, like family photos, vacation photos, etc., using Apple's iPhoto application (on a Mac), or Photoshop Album or Photoshop Elements (on a PC), or by importing them from folders. To see your photos as thumbnails, tap on any album. You can scroll through your thumbnails by swiping your finger up/down the screen. To see any photo full screen, just tap on it. Once your photo is full screen, you can see other photos in that album at that size by swiping your finger on the screen in the direction you want to scroll. If your photo bounces like it's hitting a wall, you've reached the end of that album, so swipe back in the other direction.

---

iTip: Deleting Multiple Photos from Your Camera Roll

*To delete multiple photos from your Camera Roll (to delete photos from your Photo Library or individual photo albums, you'll have to re-sync your iPhone), first tap the button that looks like an arrow coming out of a box in the top-right corner of the screen, then tap on the photos you want to delete (a red circle with a checkmark will appear on the thumbnail to let you know it's selected), then when all the ones you want to delete are selected, tap the red **Delete button** in the bottom-right corner.*

Viewing a Slide Show

Slideshow Options screen:

Transitions	Dissolve >
Play Music	OFF

Start Slideshow

Photos screen (Settings):

Photo Stream — OFF

Photo Stream automatically uploads new photos to iCloud and downloads them to all of your devices when connected to Wi-Fi.

Slideshow

Play Each Slide For	3 Seconds >
Repeat	OFF
Shuffle	OFF

HDR (High Dynamic Range)

HDR blends the best parts of three separate exposures into a single photo.

To see a slide show of your photos, tap on the Photos app to bring up the Albums screen. To see any photo album as a slide show, just tap on the album, then when the thumbnails appear, tap on one, then tap the **Play button** at the bottom of the screen. The slide shows come complete with smooth, built-in dissolve transitions between each photo, but you can choose a different type of transition on the Slideshow Options screen that appears when you tap the Play button. You can also add music here (we'll cover that next). When you're ready, tap the **Start Slideshow button**. To stop your slide show, just tap the screen once. To change the length of time each photo appears onscreen, go to the Settings app, and tap on **Photos**. Here you also have options for Repeat (to loop your slide show), and Shuffle (to play your slides in a random order). When you're done, tap the Settings button in the upper-left corner.

---

iTip: Emailing Multiple Photos

Emailing more than one photo at a time is pretty much the same process as deleting multiple photos (see the iTip on the previous page), except it works in all your photo albums. Once the photos are selected (up to five maximum), tap the Share button, then tap the **Email button** that appears. Note: If you select too many, the Email button disappears (you'll only get the Message button, where you can send up to 11 photos), so tap on any selected photo to deselect it.

Adding Background Music to Your Slide Show

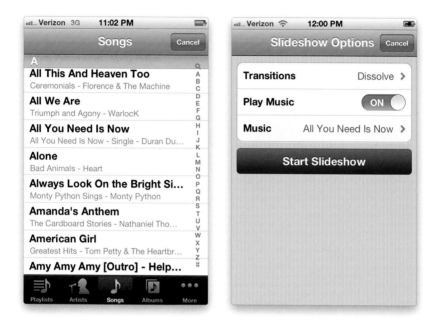

In iOS 5, there's now a slide show feature that lets you include background music. To add music to your slide show, in the Photos app, tap on the album you want to view, then tap on a photo in the album, and then tap on the Play button at the bottom center of the screen. On the Slideshow Options screen that appears, tap on the **Play Music Off button** to turn it on, then tap on the Music field that appears. This brings up your Songs list from your Music app. Just pick a song, then tap the Start Slideshow button. Your slide show will begin, and so will the music.

iTip: Pausing Your Slide Show

To pause a running slide show, just tap the screen. To start it running again, tap the Play button at the bottom center of the screen, then tap the Start Slideshow button.

Viewing and Saving Photos/Video Sent in a Text Message

If someone sends you a photo in a text message (see Chapter 3 for more on texting), you'll see a thumbnail of the photo appear in your Messages conversation. Just **tap on it** to see it full-screen size. If you decide you want to save this photo on your iPhone, tap on the full-screen photo, then tap the button in the bottom-left corner, and tap the **Save Image button** (it's saved to your iPhone's Camera Roll).

---

iTip: Copying-and-Pasting Photos

When you're looking at a photo at full-screen size, you can copy that photo into memory in case you want to paste it into another application (like an email message, or text message, etc.) by pressing-and-holding on the photo for a moment or two, and the word "Copy" will appear. Tap on that to copy the current photo into memory. Now you can paste it wherever you want (well, wherever you can normally paste stuff, anyway).

Making a Photo Your iPhone's Wallpaper

SCOTT KELBY

When you wake your iPhone from sleep, or when you're making a call, you can have a photo appear as your background image. To do this, tap on the Photos app, and when the Albums screen appears, tap on the album that contains the photo you want to use as your background wallpaper. Then, when you see the thumbnails screen appear, tap once on the photo you want to use, then tap on the button in the bottom-left corner of the screen and a list of options pops up. Tap the **Use As Wallpaper button**, and a new screen appears where you can adjust the size and position of your photo by tapping-and-dragging it around on the screen and pinching out to zoom in on the photo. When it looks good to you, choose Set, and you're set (sorry, that was lame).

---

iTip: Zooming In on a Photo

To get a closer look at any photo, either in your photo albums or a photo you've taken with the built-in camera, just tap on the photo thumbnail to see it full screen, then place your pinched fingers in the center of the screen and spread them outward to zoom in (or just double-tap on the screen). To zoom in tighter, pinch-and-spread outward once again. To return to the normal-sized view, just double-tap on the screen.

How to Email a Photo

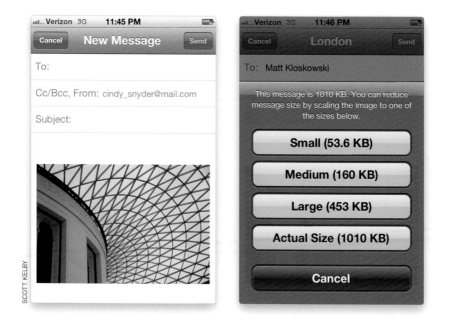

To email a photo, tap on the Photos app. If the photo you want to send is one you took with your built-in camera, tap on Camera Roll, then tap on the photo you want to email. If it's from one of your photo albums, tap on the album, then on the thumbnail of the photo you want to email. Either way, once the selected photo appears at full-screen size, tap the button on the bottom-left corner of the screen to bring up the photo options. Tap on **Email Photo**, which takes you to the New Message screen. Tap on the To field and the keyboard appears, so you can enter the email address for the person you're sending the photo to (if they're in your contacts list, tap on the blue circle on the right side of the To field). You can tap on the Cc/Bcc, From field to send a copy to someone else, and the Subject field to enter a subject line. You'll see that your photo is already included at the bottom of the email, so once that info is entered, you can email your photo by tapping the Send button in the upper-right corner of the screen. When you tap Send, you'll get a menu that asks you what size you want to send the file (larger sizes take longer to email). Choose your size, and away it goes.

📶 **iTip: Editing Photos on Your iPhone**

My favorite app for editing photos while they're still on my iPhone is Photogene (from Omer Shoor). I'm still amazed at what it's able to do (it's surprisingly powerful!).

Access Your Photos from Anywhere Using iCloud

Apple's iCloud can automatically take the photos you've taken with your iPhone and send them wirelessly to all your other devices (like your iPad, your computer, and so on). That way, your images are on all your devices all the time (how cool is that?). No more, "Oh, I wish I could show you that, but it's on my iPad" (or iPhone, or computer), because now you'll have them everywhere. Photo Stream is included in iCloud's free service. Here's how to set it up: Tap on the Settings app, then scroll down and tap on iCloud. Enter your Apple ID. Then switch on **Photo Stream**, and now the photos you take with your iPhone will be sent wirelessly to all the devices you have iCloud turned on for. There's more to iCloud than just this, so make sure you read the iCloud chapter to learn more about accessing your photos with iCloud and all the other cool things iCloud can do.

Downloading Photos from Your iPhone

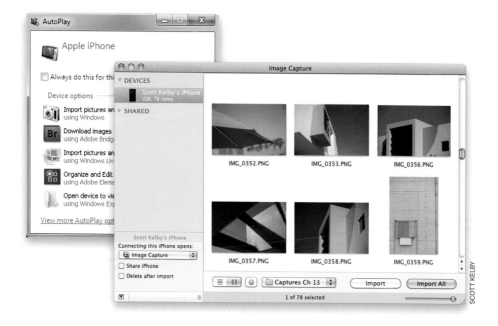

SCOTT KELBY

Although you use iTunes to manage just about everything on your iPhone, when it comes to your iPhone's camera, you treat it just like you would any other digital camera—when you connect it to your computer, if it has photos on it that you've taken, whatever software you have installed to import photos will likely launch. For example, if you're a Mac user, chances are iPhoto or Image Capture will launch and offer to import your shots. If you're a Windows user, the AutoPlay dialog or Windows Camera Wizard will kick in. You're not limited to these apps, though. You can use Photoshop Elements, Photoshop Lightroom, Apple's Aperture, Adobe Bridge's Photo Downloader, Windows Photo Gallery, or just about any other app that can bring images in from a camera. If you just want to download the images you've taken to a folder on your computer, then you can use Image Capture on your Mac or AutoPlay on your Windows PC. Both of these apps will download the images you've taken with your iPhone to a folder of your choice. From there you can do whatever you'd like with them, as they are regular JPEG files. (*Note:* You can also download them wirelessly using iCloud, as mentioned on the previous page.)

Chapter Fourteen
Cereal Killer
Killer Tips and Tricks

 This is the fifth edition of this book, and anytime we get a chance to update a book, we want to do more than just update the book with the new features—we want the new book to be better than the previous versions, because apparently we have something terribly wrong with how our brains are wired. You see, most authors are content with just updating their books, but Terry and I look at those other authors, who have things like a family life, and friends, and free time, and successful careers outside writing, and we say to ourselves, "Look at those suckers. They're out there having fun and enjoying their families when they could be indoors, tied endlessly to their laptops, typing on a keyboard, until they have nothing but bloody stumps where their fingers used to be." We laugh and poke fun at these "fun-loving" authors because clearly, they're just not "committed" enough to risk their marriages, jobs, and the occasional felony charge to really take their books to the next level. So, when Terry came up with the idea to add this chapter, even though we had already finished all the writing and updating, and the book was due to go to press, as you might imagine, it added some stress. Now, you know and I know how harmful stress can be to your health and well-being. In fact, many unlicensed physicians now feel that anxiety from writing extra tips like this can lead to stress-related health problems—in particular, cardiovascular problems that increase your risk of strokes and heart attacks—which is precisely why we named this chapter "Cereal Killer," after the song by Method Man and Redman. We considered the name "Death Trip," but only in passing.

Mirror What's on Your iPhone 4S to Your Apple TV

If you've got an iPhone 4S and an Apple TV 2 or newer with the latest software updates, you can actually mirror your iPhone's display to your Apple TV and the big screen. This is great for showing apps to a large audience or doing demonstrations. While some apps support AirPlay natively, most don't, but now you can show virtually any app on your TV. Make sure your iPhone is on the same Wi-Fi network as your Apple TV and then double-click the Home button and swipe the task bar to the right twice. This should reveal both the volume slider and the AirPlay button. Tap the AirPlay button, choose your Apple TV, and tap the **Mirroring button**, and then anything you do on your iPhone 4S should be shown on your TV. When you want to turn it off, just double-click the Home button again, swipe to the right twice, tap the AirPlay button, and choose iPhone.

Set Up a Custom Vibration Pattern

.ıll. Verizon 3G 1:37 PM		

General   Accessibility

Hearing

Custom Vibrations   **ON**

Assign unique vibration patterns to
people in Contacts. Change the default
pattern for everyone in Sounds settings.

LED Flash for Alerts   **ON**

Mono Audio   OFF

L ——————●———————— R

Physical & Motor

AssistiveTouch   Off >

Incoming calls   Default >

.ıll. Verizon 3G   1:42 PM

Settings   Sounds

New Mail   Ding >

Sent Mail   Swoosh >

Tweet   Tweet >

Calendar Alerts   Alert >

Reminder Alerts   Alert >

Lock Sounds   ON

Keyboard Clicks   OFF

Vibration Patterns

Vibration   Heartbeat >

Using the Accessibility features of iOS 5, you can now enable custom vibrations. To turn this on, in the Settings app, tap on General, and then tap on Accessibility. Under Hearing, tap to turn **Custom Vibrations** on. Now, you'll be able to change your default Vibration pattern in your Sounds settings, as well as assign custom vibration patterns to contacts in their Contacts Info screen. This is useful if you can't really tell if your iPhone is vibrating when on Silent, or if you want it to vibrate a certain way when a specific person calls.

Assign a Contact a Vibration Pattern of None

Once you've enabled Custom Vibrations (see the previous page), you can assign a contact a Vibration pattern of None. Find your contact in your Contacts list, and tap on their name to get their Info screen. Then, tap the Edit button in the top right, scroll down, and tap on Vibration. Tap on **None** at the bottom of the screen, and then tap Done twice. I use this because I leave my iPhone on at night charging on my night-stand. I have the ringer turned off, but if someone important calls, the vibration (buzzing) is enough to wake me without the loud ring. What I don't want is to receive a text message in the middle of the night, say from my bank or other business, and be woken up for something that could have waited. It's these contacts that I assign a vibration of None to. If my ringer is on, I'll hear the regular tones, but if my ringer is off and I get a text from this contact, it will be totally silent.

Use Your iPhone 4S to Dictate into Other Apps

With an iPhone 4S, you can ask Siri questions and get answers back. You can also use the speech recognition of the iPhone 4S to dictate messages or text in other apps. If you're in an app and you see a microphone icon on your keyboard, then you can tap the microphone icon and start talking instead of typing. While the iPhone 4S is pretty good at speech recognition, it doesn't automatically punctuate. You'll actually have to say the word "period" at the end of a sentence to have your iPhone 4S add a period. It works best in small bits, instead of trying to dictate long paragraphs. When you're done dictating, tap the Done button to see how well it did.

Cut, Copy, Paste, Suggest, and the Landscape Keyboard

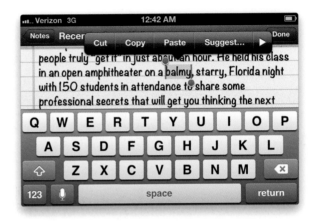

Double-tap on a word and you will get blue grab points to select what you want to copy—this can also include images, say from an email or webpage in Safari. If you double-tap where there is no word or tap-and-hold your finger on the screen for a few seconds, you get a different menu that allows you to Select (using the grab points) or Select All. Once the area you want to copy is selected, tap the Copy button. Go to the app that you want to paste this info into, tap to bring up the Paste option, and then just tap the Paste button. You can also replace words. Just double-tap on a word and, in the menu, you'll see a Suggest button if there are other words that your iPhone thinks you might want to use. Tap Suggest and then tap on the word you want to use instead. One other important feature: you can turn your iPhone sideways to get a landscape keyboard in most of your built-in apps such as Mail, Messages, and Notes.

iTip: Copying-and-Pasting Photos

You can also copy-and-paste photos from the Photos app. Just go to the album containing the photo you want to copy and tap the box with the arrow coming out of it in the top-right corner of the screen. You can tap on one or more photos to select them and then tap the Copy button at the bottom of the screen. Now, just switch to the app you want to paste the photo(s) into (like Mail), tap on the screen, and then tap the Paste button.

Master the Virtual Keyboard

When you first type on your iPhone keyboard, you'll probably want to fix your mistakes as you type, but the iPhone is smart and fixes most mistakes automatically. It compares what you're typing to the adjacent keys and usually guesses the right word, so keep typing. If you did make a mistake that you wish to fix, you don't have to delete the whole word. Tap-and-hold over the word and a magnifying glass appears. You can now slide your finger over to move the cursor to where you want to make your change or deletion. If you start typing a word that is familiar to the iPhone, it may offer a suggestion. If the suggestion is correct, hit the space bar; if it's wrong, keep typing. If you see a red underline, tap on the word to get suggestions. When you finish a sentence, there is no reason to hit period and then the space bar. If you double-tap the space bar, the iPhone will insert a period and a space, as well as enable the Shift key for the next sentence. Caps Lock is off by default, but you can turn it on in your Keyboard settings (in the Settings app, tap on General, and then tap on **Keyboard**). Once it's on in your settings, you can double-tap the Shift key to turn Caps Lock on.

---

iTip: Turning Auto-Correction Off

*You can turn off the iPhone's corrections by going to Settings, tapping on General, tapping on Keyboard, and then turning **Auto-Correction** off.*

Access Those Special Accent Characters

The next time you need to type an accent character, simply tap-and-hold on the key that would have the accent and the available accent characters will pop up. Slide your finger over to the character you want and tap it to choose it. Additional special characters are also supported. For example, if you tap-and-hold the period key, you'll get the option to insert an ellipsis (...).

iTip: Turning Off the Keyboard Clicking

*As I'm sure you've heard, the iPhone keyboard makes a clicking sound as you type, similar to that of a classic typewriter. Although I prefer to have this sound off completely (you can turn it off in the Settings, under **Sounds**), I know several people who like it. However, if you need to silence it temporarily, say in a meeting, then just turn your ringer off by moving the **Ring/Silent switch** (near the top on the left side of your iPhone) to Silent mode (move it toward the back of your iPhone).*

Switch to a Foreign Language Keyboard

To have access to multiple foreign language keyboards and be able to switch between them whenever you want, you first have to choose the ones you'll want to use. To do this, tap on the Settings app, then tap General, then tap International, then tap Keyboards, and then tap **Add New Keyboard**. This screen lists all the languages you can choose from. Tap on the keyboard(s) you want, and now when you're in an app where you need to type something, you'll see a little globe button on the bottom left of the keyboard. Just tap-and-hold on that button to switch between the keyboards you've turned on.

Enable the Emoji Keyboard

If you want to add a little graphic flavor to your text and email messages, you can enable the built-in Emoji keyboard. You turn this keyboard on in your Settings app, in the General settings. Tap on Keyboard, then tap on International Keyboards, tap on Add New Keyboard, and then scroll down and tap on **Emoji**. Once you enable it, there will be a globe icon at the bottom left of your keyboard. You can now switch between your native language keyboard and the Emoji keyboard by tapping the globe icon whenever you want to use the built-in emoticons. Tap on the buttons along the bottom to change categories, and swipe to the left to see more in that category. While it's great that we can use these, you have to keep in mind that not all operating systems will display them properly. It's probably best to stick to using these when you know you're texting another iOS user.

Sync Notes Wirelessly

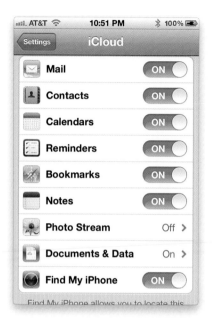

Notes can sync with iCloud or any other IMAP-based email service wirelessly. Just go to the settings for your iCloud account or any of your IMAP-based email accounts (tap on the Settings app, then tap on Mail, Contacts, Calendars) and turn on **Notes** syncing in the account settings. When you make changes either on your computer or on your iPhone, Notes will get synced back and forth wirelessly just like your contacts, calendars, and email. You can also turn this on through iTunes on your computer by clicking on your iPhone in the Devices list on the left, then in your iPhone's preferences, clicking on the Info tab. Simply turn on the **Sync Notes checkbox** (and the checkboxes for any of the other info you'd like to sync).

Tips for the International Traveler

While you might have an unlimited data plan at a set price with your carrier, all bets are off when you travel outside your country. Data roaming charges can be astronomical for simple things like checking your email. You could be getting charged for every kilobit that comes in and goes out. Luckily, there are some ways to make sure you don't come home to a bill the size of a mortgage payment. First, you have to decide if you want to be able to make calls while you travel. If so, you may need to contact your carrier and make sure that international calling is enabled on your account. The next thing you want to make sure of is that you aren't roaming on a data network. To prevent this from happening, make sure your Data Roaming is set to OFF (tap on the Settings app, then tap General, and then tap **Network**). Of course, this means that you won't be able to surf the Web, check email, etc., while you're out and about. However, you will still be able to connect to Wi-Fi networks. Let's say that you are willing to pay for data roaming, then you can turn Data Roaming on, but I recommend that you turn off Push (on the Settings screen, tap Mail, Contacts, Calendars, then tap **Fetch New Data**), so that your iPhone isn't constantly checking for new email. Also, change the Fetch setting to Manually. This way, you'll only be using data when you manually check for email, or surf the Web, or run Web-based apps.

Create Your Own Ringtones or Text Tones with GarageBand

You can make your own ringtones or text tones using Apple's GarageBand (4.1.1 or higher), which is included with iLife '11 and ships on all new Macs. To make a custom ringtone or text tone in GarageBand, launch the GarageBand application found in your Applications folder on your Mac, click iPhone Ringtone in the GarageBand new project dialog, then create a new song. Now you can either mix your own track using the software instruments, real instruments (if you're musically inclined), software loops, or vocals from your built-in or external microphone. If you're not musically inclined, you can import one of the many supported sound file formats, such as MP3. Trim your song or composition to be no longer than 40 seconds (2–5 seconds for text tones) and make sure it's set to loop. Once you have built the perfect tone, choose **Send Ringtone to iTunes** from the Share menu. Your custom ringtone or text tone will be created and will be available in your iTunes Tones Library. You can then sync it and use it on your iPhone.

Create Your Own Ringtones or Text Tones with iTunes

You may want to make a ringtone or text tone from a sound file or song in your iTunes Music Library—maybe one of your kids singing or a song from a CD (MP3s and AAC files work great)—but it takes a few steps: First, in your iTunes preferences, make sure before you import the song that your Import Using preference is set to AAC Encoder (choose Preferences from the iTunes [PC: Edit] menu, click the General icon, then click the **Import Settings button**). Listen to your song and find the 30 seconds (or less) of the song that you want (2–5 seconds for text tones) and note the segment start and end times in the progress bar at the top of the iTunes window. Choose Get Info from the File menu, click on the Options tab, enter the Start Time and Stop Time for your 30-second (or less) tone, and click OK. Choose **Create AAC Version** from the Advanced menu and this will create a 30-second version of the song, right beneath the original. Right-click on it and choose **Show in Finder (PC: Show in Windows Explorer)**. When the file appears, duplicate it and change the copy's extension from .m4a to .m4r, and then go back to iTunes and delete the 30-second version you created earlier. Now go back to the Finder window and drag the new .m4r version of your file onto the iTunes icon in your Dock (on a PC, drag it into your Tones Library) to import your new tone into your Tones Library. When you connect your iPhone to iTunes, your new tone will be available in your Tones Library to sync. Don't forget to go back and turn off the Start Time and Stop Time checkboxes for your original song, so that it will play all the way through. Here's a quick video on how to create a tone: **http://bit.ly/createaniPhoneringtone**.

Get a More Accurate Battery Status

.ıll. Verizon 3G	12:59 AM	81% ▭▪
◂ General	**Usage**	

iCloud

Total Storage	5.0 GB
Available	4.9 GB
Manage Storage	❯

Battery Usage

Battery Percentage	**ON** ⬤

Time since last full charge

Usage	1 Hour, 28 Minutes
Standby	6 Hours, 18 Minutes

On your iPhone, you can turn on a Battery Percentage display. When it's turned on, you'll see the percentage of battery charge next to the battery icon on the right side of the Status Bar at the top of your screen. Go to Settings, tap General, and then tap Usage. Here you can turn **Battery Percentage** ON or OFF.

The iPhone at Work: Enterprise Support

If your company uses Microsoft Exchange for their email, calendar, and contact serving needs, or uses Cisco VPN, you're in luck! The iPhone supports Microsoft's Active Sync and certain Cisco VPN routers for secure connections outside the firewall (currently, not all Cisco VPN routers support iPhone VPN capabilities). Depending on your IT department, they may be able to give you the settings for your Exchange account or your VPN setup, or they may have Web-based profiles that will automatically set up the iPhone for you to access your work email and other services. My company's IT department gave me a Web address that basically set up my iPhone automatically with profiles that enforce company policies, such as requiring a passcode to access the iPhone after so many minutes of inactivity. Also, if my iPhone is ever lost or stolen, I can contact our support desk and they can remotely wipe the iPhone over the air (see Chapter 7 for more on setting up a passcode and remotely wiping your iPhone). Once the wipe process starts, nothing can stop it—not even powering it down or removing the SIM card. As soon as the iPhone is powered back on, the wipe will continue. If you set up the iPhone to receive your contacts via Exchange, you'll also get access to your company's LDAP directory that you can search right on the iPhone. It's impossible to cover every thinkable corporate setup here, so my thought was to simply arm you with the information you need to go back to your IT folks and request the setup info for your iPhone. Also note that since the iPhone supports Cisco VPN, you'll be able to access things like webpages on your company's intranet from your iPhone.

Use Contact and Calendar Notes

Did you ever check in at a hotel, only to have the clerk tell you that they can't find your reservation? They ask you for your confirmation number and then you have to start digging. Why not have these little important pieces of information in the Notes field of a contact or in the Notes field of your calendar event? For example, when I'm going to take a flight somewhere, I usually block that time out on my calendar. I also put the address of the hotel and my confirmation number right in the Notes field of this event. This way, when I get to the front desk of the hotel or when I get in the back of the taxi, I'm just a couple of taps away from the information that I need. You can add these little notes either on your computer's calendar that you have syncing/pushing to your iPhone or directly on the iPhone's calendar itself. Just tap Edit in the Calendar's Event screen, and then tap the **Notes button** at the bottom. Type in any information you'll need once you get to your destination and, once you save the info, you'll be able to see it by tapping the event in your calendar.

What to Do with Your Old iPhone

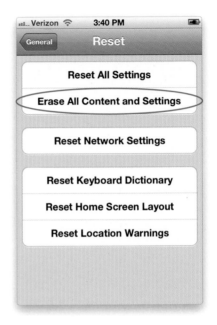

If you're upgrading to a new iPhone, then chances are you probably want to know what to do with your old iPhone. The good news is there are some great options:

Option 1: Pass it down to a family member or friend
Once you upgrade, your old iPhone can be given to someone and they'll just need to take it to a local carrier's store to get a new SIM card (if needed) and have the iPhone activated.

Option 2: Use it as an iPod touch
Since it's already activated, just with no working phone number, you can pull the SIM card out and use it as an iPod and Internet device using Wi-Fi.

Option 3: Sell it
Lastly, if you want to recoup some value out of it, you can sell it. Although the market can be somewhat flooded and there are scammers out there, too, you can fetch a fair price for your older model at places like www.nextworth.com.

Before you pass it on to someone else, though, be sure to wipe your information off of it. Tap on the Settings app, then tap General, and then tap Reset. Then just tap the **Erase All Content and Settings button**.

Restore Your Home Screen Default Layout

While it's easy to get carried away rearranging your apps from Home screen to Home screen, there may be a time that you wish to reset the main Home screen back to its original layout. To do this, just tap on the Settings app, then tap General, and then tap Reset. On the Reset screen, you'll see Reset Home Screen Layout. Tap that button and then tap **Reset Home Screen**, and you'll be back to your default layout.

---

iTip: You Can Also Clear Your iPhone in iTunes

*You can also wipe all your information off your old iPhone in iTunes by connecting it to your computer, clicking on the Summary tab in the iPhone preferences, and then clicking on **Restore** in the Version section (but the Reset option on the iPhone actually does a more secure wipe of the iPhone).*

Send Mail from a Backup Server

1:15 PM

terrywhitephotograhy | **SMTP**

Primary Server

| smtp.comcast.net | On > |

Other SMTP Servers

smtp.sbcglobal.yahoo.com	On >
smtp.macgroup.org	Off >
smtp.comcast.net	Off >
mail.terrywhite.com	Off >
namailhost.corp.adobe.com	Off >
mail.macgroup.org	Off >

If you have more than one email account, then chances are you have multiple SMTP (outgoing) email servers to choose from. Depending on the ISP (Internet service provider), you may be able to set up a backup or secondary email server to send mail from when you're on the go. For example, when I'm at home or on the road, I typically send mail from my Comcast email server. However, if their server is down, then I want to be able to send mail through either my yahoo.com server or my iCloud server. You can set up your backup email server in your iPhone's email settings. First, tap on the Settings app, then tap Mail, Contacts, Calendars. Next, tap the email account that you wish to set up with a backup SMTP server. This brings up the Account screen (you may have to tap Account to get there). Now, scroll down to **SMTP**, and tap it. You'll then get a list of additional servers that you can choose from to make your backup server. Just tap on Off to the right of any SMTP servers that you want as your backup and then tap OFF next to Server at the top to turn it on.

Create a Custom Wallpaper Image

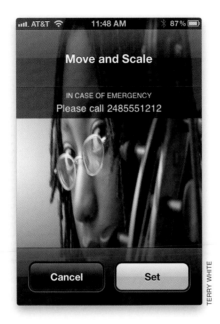

Creating a custom wallpaper image is a good way to have an ICE (In Case of Emergency) contact display on your iPhone (or your name and contact info, in case your iPhone is lost or stolen). Just put the ICE info for your emergency contact, and any other important information (such as medical conditions or allergies), right on your wallpaper image (by creating a custom image on your computer in a program like Photoshop, or taking a photo that includes your ICE or own contact info). Even if your iPhone is secured with a passcode, the information will still be displayed (you can still see part of the wallpaper when your iPhone is locked), so if something happens to you, rescue and medical personnel will know whom to contact.

---

iTip: Use an App to Create an ICE Image

There is an app called ICE (In Case of Emergency) that is available from the App Store. This app will allow you to build a custom wallpaper image from one of your existing pictures right on your iPhone. It's what I used for the wallpaper you see in the iPhone capture above.

Use Custom Home Screen Wallpaper

You can choose two different wallpaper images for your iPhone—you can choose one to be the wallpaper for your Lock screen (as shown on the previous page) and one to be the wallpaper behind all of your apps on your Home screen. Just go to Settings, tap on **Wallpaper**, and then tap the screen images to choose the images you want to use. Tap on either the Wallpaper album or one of your photo albums, choose your image, then set it, and then choose which screen you want to add it to.

Take a Screenshot

If you want to take a picture (screenshot) of something on your iPhone, there's a way to do it. Just press-and-hold the **Home button** and then press the **Sleep/Wake button** at the top right of the iPhone. The screen will flash white for a second (like a camera flash), and whatever was on your screen at the time will be saved to your Camera Roll as a PNG file. You can then email or text that file to someone, tweet it, print it, or sync/download it to your computer the next time you connect your iPhone to it.

Shake to Undo and Shake to Shuffle

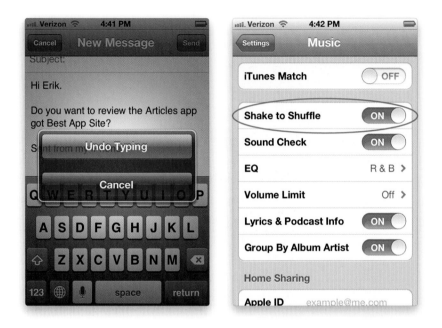

If you type something by accident, there is no Command-Z or Ctrl-Z shortcut to undo it like on your Mac or PC. However, there is a very cool way to undo on your iPhone that reminds me of the Etch A Sketch days—just shake your iPhone and, from the menu that pops up, tap **Undo Typing** to undo what you just typed. Unfortunately, shaking to undo is limited to just typing at this point. If you're listening to your Music app, you can also shake to shuffle to another song. Luckily, if you're a runner, there is a way to turn this feature off in the Music app settings (just tap on the Settings app, then **Music**).

Find Out How Much Data You're Using

If you have AT&T as your service provider, you can keep tabs on your data use to make sure you're not going over what your plan allows. Go to the Phone app, dial *DATA# (*3282#), and tap **Call**. This will trigger a text message to be sent to you updating you on your data use for your current billing cycle.

Protect Your iPhone

Password Protect It: If your iPhone is ever lost or stolen, the last thing you want to worry about is not only having to replace it, but all the information that someone will now have access to. So, tap on Settings, then on General, then on Passcode Lock. Tap on **Turn Passcode On** and set up a passcode. You'll have to enter the passcode after the time interval that you set (by tapping Require Passcode), but that's a small price to pay for peace of mind.

Buy AppleCare: If you plan on keeping your current iPhone for the length of your service contract (usually two years), then you should consider getting AppleCare. Your original Apple warranty is only for one year, and if it breaks after that, it could be expensive to fix it. AppleCare will cover it for any issues that arise that weren't caused by misuse (for example, dropping it, getting it wet, etc., are not covered).

Set Up iCloud: iCloud is a free online service Apple offers, which includes email, wireless syncing of data, online storage, and other features like Find My iPhone. Find My iPhone can not only locate your iPhone anywhere in the world, but it can also lock it and wipe it remotely, as well as display a message on it instructing the finder to return it to you. See Chapter 7 for more on Find my iPhone.

Back It Up: With all the wireless syncing that you can do, you will be tempted to sync your iPhone less via your computer. You should still connect it and sync regularly. You can also set it to back up to iCloud.

Reading ePubs and PDFs in the iBooks App

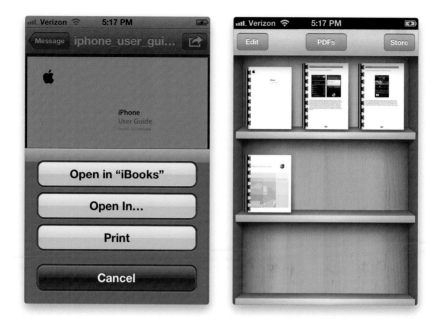

You can read ePubs and PDFs in the iBooks app (you can download it for free from the iTunes App Store) either by choosing Open in "iBooks" in a compatible app, such as Mail, or syncing them directly from iTunes and then opening them in the iBooks app. For example, let's say you receive a PDF attachment in an email. When you tap the attachment to view it, Mail will display it. However, in the upper-right corner, there'll be a button that looks like a box with an arrow coming out of it and when you tap it, you'll see a choice of apps that you have installed that can view PDFs, as well as a Print button. Tapping **Open in "iBooks"** will copy the PDF into the iBooks app, where it will appear under PDFs. Now you no longer have to dig up an email just to view the PDFs (or ePubs) you want and this is a great way to carry around your PDF manuals. If you create your own ePub in an application, like Adobe InDesign or Apple's Pages, you can view your it directly in iBooks, as well.

Why You Should Encrypt Your iPhone's Backup

iTunes offers the ability to encrypt your iPhone's backup and while you may think that it's overkill, there's a hidden benefit there. If you ever upgrade to a new iPhone or have to replace your existing one, having an encrypted backup to restore from means that iTunes will also restore your passwords in your various apps. Without an encrypted backup, iTunes (Apple) won't take the risk of restoring your iPhone's keychain data as a security precaution. For example, if someone stole your computer, they could restore your data to a different iPhone and have access to all your passwords. If your backup data is encrypted, your passwords are not restored without a password. So, in iTunes, just turn on the **Encrypt iPhone Backup checkbox** on the Summary pane and enter a password for your backup. You'll be a little safer *and* you'll have the convenience of your new iPhone being all set up with the same information, apps, and passwords that were saved on your old one.

Track Your Package

If you receive a package shipment confirmation email with a link to the tracking information, just tap the link and you'll be taken to Safari to see the tracking information.
However, if someone just emails you the tracking number and they don't link to the
shipping service's page, your iPhone will automatically detect common tracking numbers and turn them into hyperlinks. Just tap-and-hold on the tracking number in your
email, then tap the **Track Shipment button**, and it will automatically take you to the
shipper's site to track the package. This won't work for everything, but it works great
for UPS tracking numbers, in particular.

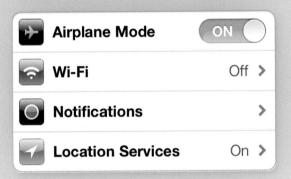

Chapter Fifteen

Setting Me Off

The Ins and Outs of Your iPhone's Settings

 I was a bit concerned about using the song title "Setting Me Off" for this chapter, because I thought it might sound too aggressive for a chapter on something as non-confrontational as learning about which iPhone settings do what. But then when I learned (by doing a quick search in the iTunes Store) that the group that recorded the song was named Speed\Kill/Hate (from their album *Acts of Insanity*), I felt much better about it. Well, that was until I noticed that the iTunes Store people had added an Explicit label beside the song's name (they do this as a warning to parents, because frankly kids couldn't care less. In fact, I imagine that when a teen sees an Explicit label beside a song, to them it means "This is for you!"). Anyway, once I saw that label, I did what any responsible adult would do—I double-clicked on it to hear the free 90-second preview. It was a heavy metal song and I have to be honest with you—I must be getting really old, because I couldn't understand a single word he sang. He could have been reading a *Sopranos* script set to music, containing every four-letter word known to merchant marines, and there is no possible way I would have been able to discern even one. Luckily, my son has a special CD player (generally used only by DJs) that lets you slow the speed of the CD down, and it was only then that I was able to hear the lyrics for the opening verse of "Setting Me Off," which were "Don't go changin'…to try and please me. You never let me down before…oooh, oooh, oooh…oooh, oooooh," so I felt pretty good about it.

Using Your iPhone on an Airplane

Most airlines won't let you have your iPhone (or any other device that transmits) on during flight. But, you'll probably want to do other stuff with it while in the air, so Apple included Airplane mode. While in this mode, the phone, Wi-Fi, Bluetooth transceivers, and GPS reception are turned off. To switch to Airplane mode, tap on the Settings app, and then tap on the word OFF next to **Airplane Mode** at the top to turn it on. You'll know you're in Airplane mode because there will be a little airplane icon in the upper-left corner where your carrier's logo used to be. Once you land, you can turn Airplane mode back off by tapping on the Airplane Mode ON button in the Settings screen.

iTip: Other Reasons to Use Airplane Mode

Although Airplane mode was designed for use on airplanes, it's also useful in other situations, such as being near a P.A. system mic, or during a recording session, or being near your stereo speakers, where there may be interference from your GSM-based iPhone. If you start to hear a loud buzzing sound coming from these other sources, it may be your iPhone causing it. Go into Airplane mode to stop it.

Connecting to Wi-Fi

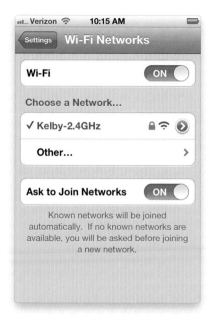

Tap on the Settings app, then tap on Wi-Fi, and turn **Wi-Fi** off or on by tapping on the ON/OFF button. You'll see the available networks that your iPhone sees and may be connected to. If there is a little Lock icon next to the network name, then that network is locked with a password (the iPhone supports both WEP and WPA security). So, if you know the password, you can type it in and log on. If there is a network that you're near that isn't broadcasting its name (it's cloaked), you can tap Other, type in the network name, and choose the type of security the network is using so that you can type in the appropriate password or HEX key. Lastly, there is an Ask to Join Networks option, and it's important to know about this one, because while you're out and about, there may be lots of Wi-Fi networks in the area. When you go to use the data features of your iPhone, if it sees an open Wi-Fi network, your iPhone will ask you to join it rather than using your carrier's 3G or EDGE network. If you find this constant asking annoying, you can turn this off. However, then it will be up to you to check to see if there is a network available.

---

iTip: On a Flight with Wi-Fi Access?

If you're on a flight that offers Wi-Fi, you can turn it back on after you've placed your iPhone in Airplane mode for takeoff and landing. Just go to the Settings app, tap Wi-Fi, then tap the available Wi-Fi network to turn it back on and connect to the in-flight wireless. Your iPhone will stay in Airplane mode, and your Phone features will still be off.

Using iTunes' Wi-Fi Sync

Before iOS 5, you always had to plug in your USB cable to your Mac or PC to sync new media and to back up your iPhone. Now, you only need to plug it in one more time, and just long enough to enable Wi-Fi Sync. In the Summary tab of iTunes, under Options, turn on the **Sync with This iPhone Over Wi-Fi checkbox**. Once you enable it, you can disconnect your iPhone (let the current sync finish first) and, from that point on, whenever you connect your iPhone to a power source, it will begin syncing with your computer via Wi-Fi. You will need to have iTunes running on your computer for Wi-Fi Sync to work. You can also initiate a wireless sync whenever you want by going into the Settings app, tapping on General, tapping on iTunes Wi-Fi Sync, and then just tapping the **Sync Now button**. It even works with more than one computer, keeping in mind that you can only sync one category (Data, Media, Photos, Apps, etc.) to one computer at a time. In my case, I sync media (music, movies, tones, books, podcasts) from my iMac and everything else from my MacBook Pro.

Twitter Settings

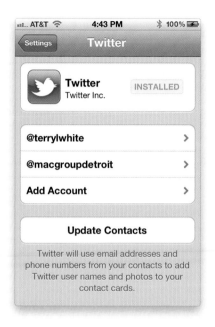

iOS 5 includes built-in Twitter support. This means that you can send tweets from various applications. For example, if you just took a photo with your iPhone camera, you can actually tweet it right from the Photos app without having to launch the Twitter app first. You can tweet a webpage that you're looking at in the Safari app just by tapping the Share button at the bottom of the Safari screen. It doesn't stop there, though, you can also tweet a video link from the YouTube app. However, before you can do any tweeting, you'll need to add your Twitter account to the Twitter settings. Just tap on the Settings app, and then tap **Twitter**. You can add your account and even add multiple accounts. Since the Contacts app now has a Twitter field, you can even tap the Update Contacts button to have the settings automatically match up your contacts' email addresses and phone numbers with their Twitter usernames, and then add their Twitter usernames and photos to their contact info on your iPhone. Although iOS 5 integrates with Twitter, it's still a good idea to download the *free* Twitter app from the App Store. There are many Twitter apps, but you should download the official Twitter app from Twitter, Inc.

FaceTime Settings

FaceTime allows you to do video chats with any other iPhone 4 or 4S, iPad 2, iPod touch, or Mac user. FaceTime works via Wi-Fi, so there is no additional cost and it doesn't chew up your data plan. By default, your iPhone uses your phone number to receive FaceTime requests. However, since FaceTime works on an iPad, iPod touch, and Mac, and there is no phone number for those devices, it uses email addresses for them, instead. In iOS 5, you can add your email addresses to your FaceTime settings on your iPhone, too. This way, if an iPad, Mac, or iPod touch user attempts to FaceTime you via your email address, you'll still get the notification. Just tap on the Settings app, then scroll down and tap on **FaceTime**. You can use your Apple ID or tap on Add An Email and add as many of your email addresses as you want.

Checking Your iPhone Usage

The Usage screen gives you a quick look at your iPhone usage (tap on the Settings app, then tap on General, and then tap on **Usage**). At the top of the Usage screen, you will see how much space your apps are taking up. You will also see how much space is being taken up by your iCloud account. You have the option of seeing the percentage of battery life left next to the battery icon at the top right of your screen. The Usage screen also lists the number of hours and minutes of usage and standby since your last full charge. This is great for tracking battery life. If you tap the Cellular Usage button, it will also show you your call time and your cellular network data usage. If you want to start tracking these statistics from scratch, just flick down to the bottom of the screen and tap the Reset Statistics button to start them over again at zero. Your Current Period call time and Cellular Network Data statistics will be reset, but your Lifetime call time and battery usage will not be.

Choosing and Managing Sounds

The Sounds screen (tap on the Settings app, then tap on **Sounds**) controls all the alert sounds your iPhone makes. You can turn your Vibrate settings on or off (by default, Vibrate is on for both the Silent and Ring modes. So even if you use the external Ring/Silent switch to turn the ringer on or off, the phone will vibrate when you receive a call). You can change the Vibrate settings for both Silent and Ring independently of each other. You can also change your Ring volume here by dragging the little knob (circle) on the slider with the speakers on both ends, and choose a default ringtone. The iPhone's default ringtone is Marimba, however, you can pick from a list of 25 different ringtones, and any custom ringtones you've added, by tapping Ringtone. The ringtone you pick is how the iPhone will ring for all incoming calls, except those of contacts that you've assigned custom ringtones to. New in iOS 5 is the ability to set custom Text Tones. You can buy new ones in the iTunes app or make your own on your computer. The iPhone makes sounds every time you receive a new text message, voicemail message, email, tweet, calendar alarm, or Reminder alert. It also makes sounds when you send email, tap on the keyboard, or when the iPhone locks. You can turn these sounds on or off individually for each area. For example, while I'm traveling, I want to leave my phone on at night for emergency calls from home, but I don't want to hear a sound from every email or text message that comes in. So I turn off the sounds for New Mail and New Text Message before I go to bed. This way, the iPhone won't make a sound unless I receive a call.

Manage Location Services Individually

There are lots of apps out there that can take advantage of your Location Services information. You can control whether or not an app has access to your location on an app-by-app basis. For example, perhaps you want to find the closest restaurant, but you don't want the pictures you take at your private home to be geotagged. No problem, just tap on the Settings app, then tap on **Location Services**, and turn on or off the ones you want to know or not know your location. If you see a little arrow next to the ON/OFF button of one of your apps, it means that particular app is using Location Services right now.

---

iTip: Turn Off Location Services to Save Battery Life

Location Services is great, however it does drain your battery faster. So, if you're not currently using any location-aware apps, then go ahead and turn off Location Services (at the top of the Location Services settings screen) to save power.

Adjusting the Brightness

The iPhone screen is very bright, and it automatically adjusts under certain conditions to conserve battery life. But, if you want to manually adjust the brightness, you can. Tap the **Brightness button** in the Settings screen and drag the slider to the left to make the screen dimmer or to the right to make it brighter. You can also turn off Auto-Brightness if you like by tapping on the ON/OFF button.

Changing Your Wallpaper

When you first turn on your iPhone or wake it from sleep, it displays a photo of water droplets on a gray background. But, if you want to choose a different picture, tap the **Wallpaper button** in the Settings screen. You'll have a choice between the Apple-supplied wallpaper photos in the Wallpaper screen or your own photos that you either took with your iPhone camera or synced from your computer. Find the photo you want to use as your wallpaper and tap on it. You'll be able to resize it using two fingers and move it around. Once it looks the way you want, tap the Set button. You'll also have the choice of setting it for your Lock Screen, Home Screen, or both. This means that you can have two different wallpaper images: one for your Lock screen and one as the background for your Home screens.

Your iPhone's General Settings

In the General settings screen in the Settings app, tapping **About** gives you almost all the information you could need about your iPhone. You'll find things like the number of songs, videos, and photos that you have, as well as the amount of available space, serial number of your iPhone, software version, and firmware version. You'll also find the MAC addresses for the Wi-Fi and Bluetooth chips. You'll find a button to turn **Bluetooth** on and pair it with your headset or car kit, and in the **Keyboard** screen, you'll be able to turn on the Enable Caps Lock function (boy was I happy to find that one). You can even set up a four-digit password that would have to be typed in to unlock your iPhone. For those needing to set up a VPN (Virtual Private Network) connection to access their corporate network, you would do that on the **Network** screen (you'll need the VPN settings from your company's IT department). Lastly, if you have a teenager with an iPhone, you can set up some restrictions here by tapping Restrictions. See Chapter 10 for more on Restrictions settings.

Updating Your Software Over the Air

iOS 5 introduces the ability to update your iPhone operating system software over the air. This means that when Apple updates the iOS, you don't have to plug in your iPhone to your computer to update it. The updates are now smaller, so you can even do many of them via a cellular network. To check to see if you have a Software Update pending, just tap General in the Settings app, and then tap **Software Update**.

Manage Your Push Notifications

iOS 5 has made great enhancements to push notifications, including a new Notifications Center. It's where an app sends you a notification without it actually having to be running in the foreground. For example, the CNN app can pop up a message when there is a breaking news story; the Facebook app can alert you when someone just tagged you in a photo; the Google Voice app can let you know that you just received a message; etc. You can choose to get a Sound, a Badge, a Banner, an Alert, or any combination of those, or turn it off altogether. You can control how each app notifies you in the Notifications settings, including whether or not it appears on the Lock screen (tap on the Settings app, then tap on **Notifications**). For example, if someone posts a message on my Facebook wall, it's not an emergency—it can wait. I don't want to see a Banner or Alert every time that happens. If I leave Badge App Icon on, then I'll just get a numeric badge over the Facebook app icon on my Home screen, letting me know how many alerts I've missed. In most cases, you can turn on/off each type of notification for each app. To get to the Notifications Center and see all your notifications, just swipe down from the top of any screen.

---

iTip: See Weather Forecast

If you have the Weather displaying at the top of your Notifications Center, you can swipe to the left or right to see the forecast.

Control Your Spotlight Searches

You can control your search results better when using the global Spotlight search feature. Tap on the Settings app, then General, and then tap on **Spotlight Search**. Here, you can not only check and uncheck the categories you want searched, but more importantly, you can reorder them in the priority that you want the results to show (by just tapping on the three bars to the right of any search option and dragging it where you want it). For example, I rarely use this feature to search for music (or other Music app or Videos app items), and I don't want those results to show first, so I moved Music, Podcasts, Videos, and Audiobooks lower in the list (if I'm searching for "Scott," I'm probably looking for a contact named Scott and not Jill Scott. :)

Don't Forget to Set Your Time Zone

If you travel to different time zones, you'll have to decide how you want your iPhone to handle the times for events in your calendar. For example, let's say you have an appointment set for 12:00 p.m. Eastern time. When you go to California, which is on Pacific time, do you want the event to display as 12:00 p.m. or 9:00 a.m.? If you leave Time Zone Support off, then the event will automatically adjust based upon the time zone you're in. So, your appointment would display as 9:00 a.m. If you want it to display the time you set the appointment for, no matter what time zone you're in, then you would turn Time Zone Support on and set your home/default time zone. Tap on the Settings app and then tap Mail, Contacts, Calendars. Scroll down to the Calendars section and tap **Time Zone Support**. By default, Time Zone Support is on (if you wanted to turn it off, tap on ON). Tap Time Zone and type in your home/default city. If you live in a smaller town, it may not be in the list, so you may have to choose the largest city in your time zone instead. In case you were wondering, I prefer this setting to be off—I want the appointment to be in the local time wherever I am.

Your Mail, Contacts, Calendars Settings

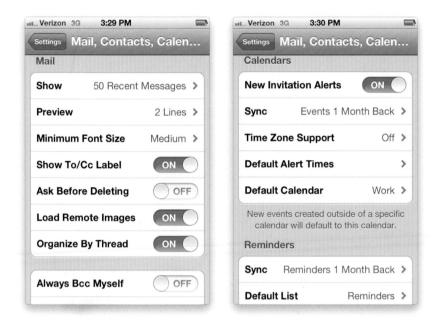

In the Mail, Contacts, Calendars screen in the Settings app, you can see, change, or add email accounts. However, you can also change the settings for the way the iPhone works with your existing email accounts, contacts, and calendars. By default, the iPhone shows you the 50 most recent messages, which you can change to 100, 200, 500, or 1,000. It also shows you the first two lines of the incoming message without having to open the message, which you can change from zero to five lines. You can also choose your minimum font size here. This is important for those that have a hard time reading the smaller screen of the iPhone. You can turn on Show To/Cc Label of your incoming messages, which will put a little To or CC in front of your name to let you know if the message was sent to you or you were just copied on it. When you delete a message on your iPhone, it does it immediately. However, if you'd like a warning, you can turn on Ask Before Deleting. You can have images received in emails load manually or automatically by turning Load Remote Images on or off. Turning on Organize By Thread keeps all replies from a single email together, as if in a subfolder for that email message. If you want to have Mail always blind copy you on your outgoing messages, you can turn on Always Bcc Myself. The iPhone puts a cool "Sent from my iPhone" message at the end of every email that you send out and you can edit this by tapping Signature. You can also choose how your contacts are displayed and sorted. If you're upgrading from a different kind of phone that stores the contacts on the SIM card, you can import those contacts. This is the screen that also lets you set options for your calendar and reminder alerts and how far back to sync events that have passed.

Your Phone App Settings

In the Phone settings, within the Calls section, you can enable Call Forwarding to have your incoming calls automatically forwarded to another number. Call Waiting can be turned off, so that if you're on a call and another call comes in, it will be sent to voicemail immediately. You can also turn off the Show My Caller ID feature. However, keep in mind that many people don't accept calls from numbers that are blocked. (*Note:* These options are for AT&T service, and may vary if you have a different service provider—see Verizon's options above right.) For the hearing impaired, you can turn on the TTY (Teletypewriter) feature, and Apple does sell an iPhone TTY adapter separately that allows you to connect your iPhone to teletype machines. Depending on your service provider, you may be able to change your voicemail password here, as well. Next is a feature called International Assist that will automatically add the appropriate numbers to your calls back home when you're traveling abroad. The last two options are SIM PIN and Services for your provider. Enabling a SIM PIN makes it harder for someone to take your SIM card and use it in another phone. If your provider uses the Services option, you'll be able to access things like speed dial numbers to check your bill balance and directory assistance.

Safari Web Browser Settings

Using the Safari settings screen, you can change your default search engine. Whether you prefer Google search, Yahoo search, or Bing search, you can change that here. There is a Fraud Warning setting (by default, it's on). This will help warn you if you visit a site that is known to be compromised by malicious code. By default, the iPhone also has JavaScript and Block Pop-Ups on. You can turn each of these off if you need to. Safari is set to accept cookies from visited sites. Other than Never, this is probably the safest setting. Cookies are good in the fact that they minimize the need on many sites to have to constantly log in. Your login info or site settings can be stored as a cookie right in your iPhone's Safari browser. In this screen, you can also choose to clear your browsing history, and Clear Cookies and Data to remove any trace of your having been to the sites you've been to. You can also turn on the AutoFill setting near the top of the Safari screen, so that when you visit sites that require you to type in passwords or other information, such as your address, you can just tap the AutoFill button to have those pieces of info automatically filled in.

Your Messages App Settings

iOS 5 brings a new feature to Messages called iMessage. When iMessage is on (it is by default and is found on the Messages screen), your Messages app will automatically detect if you're sending a text or picture message to another iOS 5 user and send it via iMessage instead of your cellular carrier's SMS system. The main benefit here is that iMessages don't count against your SMS/text message plan, especially if you're on a limited one. You can turn on Send Read Receipts, so that others will know when you've read their message. The next option is Send As SMS. This is on by default and will send your message as a regular SMS/MMS to a user when iMessage fails. Tap on Receive At to add your email address(es) that you want to be able to receive iMessages at, too. This way, a user can send you an iMessage without having to know your phone number. With Group Messaging on (by default, near the bottom), when you send a message to a group of people and they reply, the reply will go to everyone in the group.

Your Music App Settings

There are some cool settings for the Music app (found in the Settings app, under Music): The first two are for the new iTunes Match. iTunes Match is an optional paid service ($24.99/year) that allows you to have all of your music synced to iCloud and streamed to your iPhone. The next one allows you to shake your iPhone to shuffle your songs. Next, is Sound Check and with this on, your iPhone's Music app attempts to balance the sound levels of your songs. So, for example, if you have one song that is really loud and another song that isn't so loud, with Sound Check on it should lower the volume of the really loud song and raise the volume of the song that isn't so loud. The next setting is for EQ (equalizer). It's possible (and recommended) to set the EQ setting for each of your songs in iTunes on your computer. You can set all your rock tracks to the Rock EQ setting, all your R&B to the R&B EQ setting, all your jazz to the Jazz EQ setting, etc. When they are played on the iPhone, they'll sound better. But, you can also set a default EQ setting on your iPhone for the songs that don't have an EQ setting. You can only pick one, so pick the one that would cover most of your music collection. Next, you can set a volume limit. This will limit the volume across the board, and there's even a four-digit security code that you can assign to it so your teenager can't go back in and just turn it off. With Lyrics & Podcast Info on, you can tap a song's album artwork to see its lyrics, if you've added them in iTunes on your computer, or tap on a podcast you're playing to get information about what's in that podcast. At the bottom is the Home Sharing section, which gives you access to your music from your computer running iTunes over your Wi-Fi network.

Your Videos App Settings

Settings   Video

Start Playing   Where Left Off ›

Closed Captioning   ⚪ OFF

Home Sharing

Apple ID   terry

Password   •••••••••

An Apple ID is required to use Home Sharing.

In iOS 5, Apple split out your videos and music from a single app called iPod to two apps: Music and Videos. The Videos app is where you go to play any video content stored on your iPhone, such as movies, TV shows, video podcasts, and music videos. The Video settings are pretty straightforward. The first setting is to play videos from where you left off as opposed to starting from the beginning each time, and the second one is to turn on Closed Captioning or not, if the video has closed captioning in it. You also have a Home Sharing section, which allows you to stream videos from your computer running iTunes over your Wi-Fi network.

Your Photos App Settings

There are five basic settings for the Photos app (found in the Settings app). The first setting is for Photo Stream. Photo Stream is part of Apple's free iCloud service (for more on iCloud, see Chapter 9). With Photo Stream on, the photos you take with your iPhone will automatically be synced to iCloud and then made available on your other devices that have Photo Stream, such as an Apple TV, an iPad, or a Mac running iPhoto. It syncs your 1,000 most recent photos or anything less than 30 days old. The next setting lets you set the duration for each photo during your slide shows. The default is 3 seconds, but you can set it from 2 to 20 seconds. The third setting is Repeat. By default, this is off, which means that your slide show will stop after the last slide. You can turn on Repeat so that it loops the slide show. The next setting is Shuffle, which is off by default. With Shuffle on, your slide shows will play in a random order. Lastly, your iPhone 4 or 4S can create HDR (High Dynamic Range) photos. This setting lets you keep both the HDR and regular photo, or not.

Your Notes App Settings

The Notes app is pretty handy for jotting down notes on the go. If you have an iPhone 4S, you can even dictate them. And, now, you can also change the default font to one that's easier to read for you (from the Notes screen). More importantly, if you have more than one email account that supports Notes, you can choose a default email account to sync your Notes with. This is handy when you want to create notes in one place (say your computer) and read them in another place (say your iPhone). *Note:* This may not be available on all carriers.

iTunes Store Settings

If you tap on the Settings app, then tap on **Store**, you can turn on Automatic Downloads, so that any Music, Apps, or Books that you purchase on your computer or other iDevice will be automatically downloaded to your iPhone. The next option is to turn on or off cellular data for your downloads. If you have a limited data plan, you may want to turn this off so that your iTunes downloads only happen when you're connected to Wi-Fi. If you have any apps that can automatically download content, such as newspaper or magazine apps, you'll be able to control them individually here. At the bottom, you'll see your Apple ID. You can tap it to sign out or switch user accounts.

Downloaded App Settings

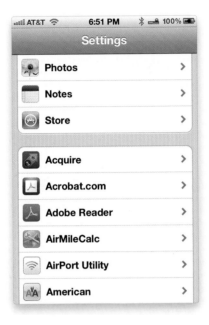

If you have any downloaded apps on your iPhone, the developer may have included some settings that you can change. These apps will be at the bottom of the main Settings screen. Just tap the app that you wish to adjust. If you delete the app, the settings for that app will also be deleted.

Using Your iPhone to Connect Your Laptop or Other Wi-Fi Device to the Internet

This is called a Personal Hotspot, and it allows you to use your iPhone's 3G data connection to provide Internet access to your laptop (or other Wi-Fi-enabled device). You can connect to your iPhone via Wi-Fi, Bluetooth, or USB (using your sync cable). In order for you to use a Personal Hotspot, your carrier must support it, and they may charge you an additional monthly fee to use it. Once you have a Personal Hotspot plan on your account, the **Personal Hotspot** setting on the Network settings screen (in the General settings) should become active. Just turn it on and connect your iPhone to your laptop. Once you're connected, a blue band will appear at the top of the iPhone screen (as seen on the right above). If your laptop has Wi-Fi or Bluetooth, then this will let you connect to the Internet from wherever you have 3G data coverage without even having to take your iPhone out of your pocket or purse. Bluetooth is rated for distances up to 30 feet. *Note:* AT&T has Personal Hotspot support for the iPhone. However, you'll have to make a choice: if you're currently grandfathered in from a previous iPhone and have an unlimited data plan, you *cannot* sign up for this without giving up that unlimited plan. As of the writing of this book, you'll have to go with the DataPro plan, which has a 4-GB-per-month cap on it for $45/month.

Choose to set up as a new iPhone
or restore from a backup.

Set Up as New iPhone

Restore from iCloud Backup ✓

Restore from iTunes Backup

Chapter Sixteen

The Trouble with Boys

Troubleshooting Your iPhone

Terry asked me to write this chapter intro for two reasons: (1) it's my job to write the chapter intros, and (2) I'm not really qualified to write anything in a troubleshooting chapter. It's only because nothing has gone the slightest bit wrong with my iPhone since I bought it, so I've never had an occasion to troubleshoot a problem. On the other hand, Terry (being a renown gadget guru and committed iPhone freak) is very hard on technology. It's not unusual to stop at Terry's house and find him taking some new gadget (like an iPhone) and exposing it to harsher conditions than your average user is likely to experience (unless he or she were to lead an expedition to Antarctica, or do so many bad things that they wind up in "the really hot place" where really bad people go—you know where I'm talking about: Phoenix). Anyway, Terry asked me to write this intro, and I have to tell you, I'm honored to do it. In fact, I'm honored to be sharing the pages of this book with him, because even though many people don't know this, Terry is the reigning Midwest freestyle clogging champion (in the men's 35–45 age bracket), and he competes nationwide at clogging conventions, state fairs, and competitions, including Clogapalooza 2012 where he took third place in the men's individual freestyle competition. I was there cheering Terry on, and I've got to tell you—he was robbed. One of the judges worked for Microsoft and, not coincidentally, was the only one to score Terry's performance as an 8.2 (all the other judges scored him as a 10). What a shame—we really thought it was "his year."

Dropped Calls and Bad Reception

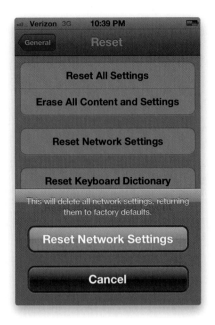

Depending on your carrier and physical location, you may just be in a bad reception area. But, if you feel that it's happening more often than it should, here are some things to remember: Your iPhone 4 or 4S has antennas along the sides of the phone. Many are saying that physical contact (i.e., your hand) covering the little black strips on the sides will lower your reception. If you're having issues, you may want to invest in a case or Apple's iPhone 4 Bumper cover to help reduce this issue (it may be *free* to you depending on when you bought your iPhone 4). Also, make sure that you've got the latest software update for your iPhone (go to your Settings app and, under General, tap on **Software Update**). Another thing to try is resetting your Network settings (under General settings, under Reset at the bottom, tap on **Reset Network Settings**). Some find this instantly fixes their problems. Please note that when you do this, it will also blow away any saved Wi-Fi passwords.

---

iTip: Getting Better Reception on an iPhone 4

*Simply try turning 3G off. I know that it may sound like a really bad thing. But, if you're not actively surfing the Web or checking email, then having 3G on is not really helping you. So try turning it off to see if that improves your reception in troubled areas by tapping on the Settings app, then tapping General, and then tapping Network. Tap the **Enable 3G ON/OFF button** to turn 3G off. (Note: This setting is not available on the iPhone 4S.)*

The Quick Fix for Most Problems

Most problems can be fixed by simply turning your iPhone off and back on again. To turn it off and back on, hold down the **Sleep/Wake button** on the top. After a few seconds, you will get a message that says Slide to Power Off. Go ahead and tap-and-hold on the red arrow button, then slide your finger across to the right to power it off. Once it powers off, you can power it back on by holding down the Sleep/Wake button, again. Once your iPhone comes back on, you can try to do whatever it was that wasn't working before.

Your iPhone Doesn't Come On or Respond

Make sure that your battery is charged—try either connecting it to your computer's
USB port or to the AC adapter with the USB cable that came with your iPhone. Its screen
should come on when it's connected to a power source and indicate that the battery
is charging. If not, then you may want to try rebooting it. Press-and-hold the **Home
button** and the **Sleep/Wake button** located on the top of the iPhone until you see
the Apple logo. You can let go then and should be back in business. If your iPhone
is on but not responding to your touch, you can also try rebooting it the same way.
Your iPhone should boot up normally and return to normal operation.

---

iTip: Use the USB Cable That Came with Your iPhone

*Make sure you use the USB cable that came with your iPhone 4 or 4S, as older cables and
chargers may not be compatible. Also, older FireWire-based chargers will not charge the
iPhone 3G or later, or 2nd generation or later iPod touch.*

No Sound

There could be several reasons why your iPhone isn't making any sounds. The first thing to check is that you don't have it on Silent, so check the **Ring/Silent switch** on the left side of the iPhone and make sure it's pushed toward the front of the iPhone. If you see an orange bar on the switch, that means that it's on Silent. The next thing to check is the volume. Press the **Volume Up button** on the left side of the iPhone below the Ring/Silent switch (the Ring/Silent switch and the Volume Up and Down buttons are shown circled above). If you're not hearing anything, then check to make sure the volume is turned up in your app, as well. Make sure there isn't anything plugged into the headset jack, or if you are using headphones, that they are pressed all the way in. Most headphones will not go all the way down into the recessed headset jack. Finally, if you have your iPhone docked in an iPod or iPhone speaker system, make sure that the speaker system has power and is on.

You're on Wi-Fi, but Your iPhone Uses 3G

First, make sure your password has been entered correctly by tapping the Settings app, then tapping Wi-Fi. Tap the blue arrow button next to the name of your network and then tap **Forget This Network**. Try accessing your Wi-Fi network again and re-entering the password. If the WEP password doesn't work, try entering the HEX key. If your router uses MAC address filtering, then you'll need to log onto your router's admin page and enter the iPhone's Wi-Fi address, which can be found on the **About** screen under General settings.

Renew Your DHCP Lease Manually

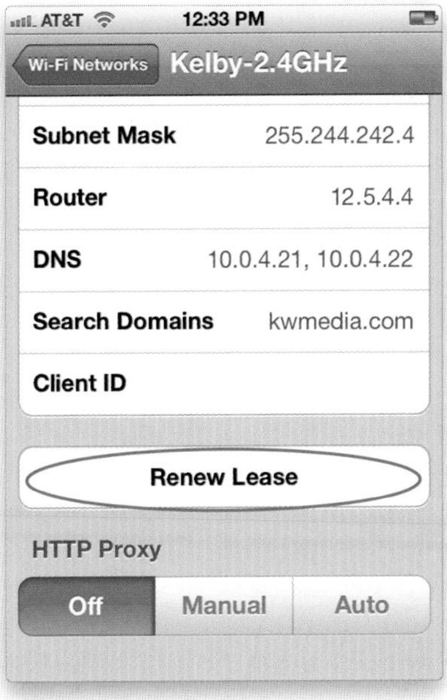

.ıll. AT&T 📶	12:33 PM	🔋
◀ Wi-Fi Networks **Kelby-2.4GHz**		

Subnet Mask	255.244.242.4
Router	12.5.4.4
DNS	10.0.4.21, 10.0.4.22
Search Domains	kwmedia.com
Client ID	

Renew Lease

HTTP Proxy

Off	Manual	Auto

If you're connected to a commercial Wi-Fi hot spot, say at a favorite coffee shop or restaurant, and you're having problems getting onto the Internet, try renewing your DHCP lease. Tap on the Settings app and then tap Wi-Fi. Next, tap the blue arrow button for the network that you're connected to, scroll down, and tap the **Renew Lease button**. This will tell the iPhone to grab an updated IP address, and possibly updated DNS info.

Get a Fresh Start with Your Information

If you want to wipe the Contacts, Calendars, Bookmarks, Notes, or Mail Accounts settings from your iPhone and replace them with what's currently on your computer, you can do this in iTunes. After you connect your iPhone to your computer, click on the Info preferences tab after you click on your iPhone in the Devices list. In the Advanced section, there is a checkbox for each of the items just mentioned that you can turn on to have iTunes overwrite what's currently on the iPhone with what's on your computer. This will be a one-time thing and your iPhone will sync normally the next time you connect it.

Wiping Your iPhone Completely

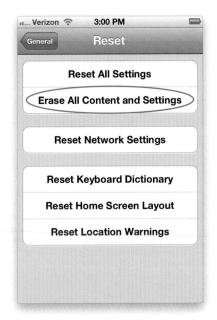

If you want to start completely from scratch on your iPhone and reset it back to its factory defaults, tap on the Settings app, then tap General. You will see a **Reset button** at the bottom of the General screen. Tap Reset and you can choose to Reset All Settings, Erase All Content and Settings, Reset Network Settings, Reset Keyboard Dictionary, Reset Home Screen Layout, or Reset Location Warnings. The two main ones that you'll want to choose from are Reset All Settings and Erase All Content and Settings. The first choice (Reset All Settings) will reset all your settings and preferences but leave your data and media intact, so you will still have all your contacts, calendars, songs, etc. The second option (Erase All Content and Settings) is the one that will reset your iPhone back to its factory defaults and wipe out everything you put on it.

Can't Make Calls

If you want to make a call, your iPhone has to be active and there has to be a cellular network in range. Your carrier's name should be displayed in the upper-left corner, along with your current signal strength. If you're roaming on another provider's network, you should see that network's name. If you don't see a network name or you see No Service, then you will not be able to make calls until you are back in the range of a wireless carrier. Also, if you have traveled outside of your country's home network, you may not be set up for international roaming. Check with your carrier to make sure that your account has international roaming. Also, make sure you're not in Airplane mode. If there is a little icon of a plane in the upper-left corner of the screen, then you are in Airplane mode and will not be able to make calls until you turn it off in the Settings app.

📶 **iTip: Your iPhone Can Cause Interference**

If you have other wireless devices in your home/office, such as cordless phones, speaker systems, video/audio recording equipment, etc., the iPhone's transceiver could cause audible interference (buzzing) on them. You can usually cure it by going to Settings and turning on **Airplane Mode**. *However, note that while your iPhone is in Airplane mode, you will not be able to make or receive calls or texts, or access the Internet.*

When I Sync, My New Apps Get Deleted

If you bought/downloaded a new app on your iPhone, and noticed that sometimes when you sync with your computer, the app is deleted from your iPhone, you may have accidentally told iTunes to do this. The first time you sync and iTunes sees purchased content that is not in the iTunes Library, you'll get a dialog asking if you want to transfer those purchases (yes, including apps) to your computer. If you click No and, more importantly, turn on the Don't Show This Again checkbox, from that point on, iTunes will not transfer any new items. Of course, since syncing creates a mirror of what's in iTunes on your iPhone, it has no choice but to remove the app(s). But, you can reset this warning (and all others) in your iTunes preferences (Command-, [comma; PC: Ctrl-,]), under the Advanced tab, by clicking the **Reset Warnings button**. The next time you sync, you should be asked if you want to transfer purchases, and this time click Yes.

Did Your App Crash?

Not all apps are created equally, so you may have an app crash now and then. The good thing is that the iPhone operating system (iOS) is based upon Mac OS X, which is really reliable. So even if an app crashes, it usually won't affect the rest of the iPhone and will simply return you to the Home screen. However, if the app just appears frozen and not responding, then you can manually force quit it by pressing-and-holding the **Sleep/Wake button** at the top of the iPhone until the red button with "Slide to Power Off" appears. Then press-and-hold the **Home button** on the front of the iPhone for at least six seconds, and you should be returned to the Home screen.

Quit an App Manually

If you have an app that isn't frozen, but appears to be running poorly, or you just want to start it up from a cold start, then you'll need to manually quit it. Double-click the Home button to bring up the multitasking bar. Scroll along the bar (by swiping side-ways) until you see the app that you want to quit, and then press-and-hold on it like you're rearranging your apps on your Home screen. All of the apps in the multitasking bar will start to wiggle, and a – **(minus sign) button** will appear in the upper-left corner of each one. Just tap that button on the app you want to quit. Now you can press the Home button again and relaunch the app, if you like.

Do a Backup and Restore

If your iPhone is misbehaving or just plain acting weird, it may be time to do a restore. You'll need to sync your iPhone before doing this so that it is backed up. Once the sync is done, leave your iPhone connected to your computer and click the **Restore button** on the Summary pane in your iPhone's preferences in iTunes. This will reinstall the current iPhone firmware on your iPhone and then do a restore of your data from the backup. This can easily take 20 minutes or more, so make sure you do it when you have time to be without your iPhone.

Missing Album Art

You can download album art for most of your iTunes Music Library right in iTunes. Just go to the Advanced menu and choose **Get Album Artwork**. If you notice a bunch of missing album art in iTunes or on your iPhone, you can fix this in iTunes by selecting the tracks that are missing album art, then Right-clicking on them and choosing **Clear Downloaded Artwork**. Right-click on them again and choose **Get Album Artwork**. iTunes will then download the album art for any tracks you are missing artwork for that it has in its catalog. Finally, re-sync your iPhone.

Battery Saving Tips

Your iPhone's battery life is going to depend on how you use it. Any one of these tips will help, but the more of them you use, the longer your battery will go between charges.

Keep your iPhone out of the sun. This is one of the most important things you can do to conserve battery life. Heat will affect your battery the most, so try not to leave it in any hot places, like your car's glove box.

Try reducing the screen brightness. The screen is one of the main sources for drawing power. If you reduce the brightness, the iPhone will use less battery power. You can do this from the Settings screen.

Turn off Wi-Fi and Bluetooth, if not needed. If you're in an area that doesn't have Wi-Fi, or you're traveling in and out of hotspots, then there is no reason to have your iPhone constantly searching for a network to connect to. Turn off Wi-Fi from the Settings screen. If you're not using your Bluetooth headset, you can turn that off, too (from the General settings screen). With these radios off, the iPhone will also charge faster.

Let your battery run completely down. As with most electronic devices that use rechargeable batteries, it's always a good idea to let your battery run completely down occasionally before recharging. Think of it as exorcising the battery and prolonging its life, as well.

More Battery Saving Tips

ᵃᵗᵗ Verizon 📶 3:56 PM 🔋	**ᵃᵗᵗ Verizon 📶 3:57 PM 🔋**
◀ Mail... **Fetch New Data**	◀ Settings **Location Services**
Push ◯ OFF	**Location Services** ◯ OFF
New data will be pushed to your iPhone from the server.	Location Services uses GPS along with crowd-sourced Wi-Fi hotspot and cell tower locations to determine your approximate location.
Fetch	
The schedule below is used when push is off or for applications which do not support push. For better battery life, fetch less frequently.	
Every 15 Minutes	
Every 30 Minutes ✓	
Hourly	
Manually	

Here are a couple more options to save battery life: If you have an iPhone 4 and you're not actively surfing the Web, then having the 3G feature turned on is putting an unnecessary drain on your battery. Tap on the Settings app, and then tap General. Next tap Network, and then tap the **Enable 3G ON/OFF button** to turn it off (this is not available on the iPhone 4S). Also, if you're having your data (such as email, and calendar and contact updates) "pushed," then you can switch from Push to Fetch. This will bring in your data on a timed interval, as opposed to every second of the day. I found that turning off Push gave me a drastic improvement on my iPhone's battery life. You can turn Push off by tapping Settings and then tapping Mail, Contacts, Calendars, then **Fetch New Data**. Lastly, if you don't need the location services (geotagging your photos, GPS, etc.), you can also extend your battery life by turning **Location Services** off in the General settings.

iPhone Not Seen by iTunes

To sync your iPhone to iTunes, you need to have iTunes version 9.2 or higher. If you're a Mac user, you also need to at least be on Mac OS X Tiger (version 10.4.11 or higher, or version 10.5.8 or higher to sync Notes or use the iPhone as a modem). There needs to be enough battery power for the iPhone to be able to turn on—if the iPhone's battery is completely drained, charge it for at least 10 minutes before attempting to sync it in iTunes. If that doesn't work, try plugging the iPhone into a different USB 2 port on your computer. If you're trying to use it with a USB hub, you may want to see if it works connected directly to your computer first and also try disconnecting other USB devices. If that doesn't work, try turning your iPhone off and back on before connecting to your computer. Lastly, try re-installing iTunes to make sure that it has what it needs to see mobile devices.

SIM Card Not Detected by Your iPhone

SIM tray

SIM tray

iPhone 4 or 4S   *iPhone 3GS*

The iPhone is a GSM-based phone, so it comes with a SIM card already installed in it. If your iPhone isn't seeing the SIM card, try removing it and re-seating it. Using a small paper clip (or the SIM card removal tool that came with your iPhone 3G or 3GS; it was attached to the folder containing your Information Guide, etc.), insert one end in the hole on the SIM tray and press firmly until the tray pops up. Make sure there is no dirt or debris on it and try putting it back in. The SIM tray on the iPhone 4 and 4S is located on the side; on the iPhone 3GS, it's located on the top. *Note:* The iPhone 4 and 4S use a Micro SIM card, so it's not compatible with regular SIM slots unless you have an adapter tray. You can get an adapter tray on Amazon.com, if you ever need to put your SIM card in another phone.

📶 iTip: Remove Your SIM Card When Servicing

If you ever have to send your iPhone in for service, you can remove the SIM card and try it in another GSM-based phone (this way, you'll still have use of a cell phone while yours is being serviced. But, as I mentioned above, you'll need an adapter tray if you have an iPhone 4 or 4S). Apple doesn't require your SIM card to service your phone and, as a matter of fact, they request that you remove it before you send it in anyway.

Software Updates Are Important

Every now and then, problems will be addressed in software updates for both your iPhone and your apps. If you're experiencing problems, make sure you're on the latest version of your iOS, and that you've updated your apps to their latest versions. To check for iOS updates, tap on the Settings app, then tap on General, and tap on **Software Update**. To check for app updates, tap on App Store on the Home screen, and then tap on **Updates** at the bottom right.

Index